Sshhhh....

Other Books by Linda Tatelbaum

CARRYING WATER AS A WAY OF LIFE:
A Homesteader's History
(1997, nonfiction)

WRITER ON THE ROCKS—
Moving the Impossible
(2000, nonfiction)

YES & NO: PARIS 1969
(2004, fiction)

woman who speaks tree

Confessions of a Tree Hugger

Linda Tatelbaum

About Time Press
Appleton, Maine

Woman Who Speaks Tree is a work of nonfiction. A few names have been changed, but most have not.

Gary Snyder's "Earth Verse" quoted in full by permission of Perseus Group.

The history of Rockland Jews, the Adas Yoshuron Synagogue 75th year book (1987).

Quotes from Thoreau, *Ktaadn* (Tanam Press) and "Walking" (Dover).

Portions of the following have appeared previously: "Paper Scissors Rock" in *The Maine Scholar* ; "Holy Kitchen" in *Maine Voices, Living on Earth* (Public Radio International), *Maine Things Considered* (Maine Public Radio Network); "The College and the Woods" in *Colby*.

ISBN 978-0-9654428-6-2
Library of Congress Control Number 2008905885

Printed and manufactured in Maine, USA
Cover design by Ribeck & Co, Inc.
Cover art (and title) by Robert Shetterly
Text design by Lurelle Cheverie
Author photo by Noah T. Winer
Other photos by: Kathleen Dooher [page 32]; Harold Winer [40]; Kal Winer [48]; Bonnie Farmer [69]; Paul Comisar [114]; Karli Jaffe [121]; Adam Musial [130].

ABOUT TIME PRESS
1050 Guinea Ridge Road
Appleton, Maine 04862
(207) 785-4634
www.colby.edu/~ltatelb

Thank You

TO you, reader, for supporting About Time Press. Without you, we're history.

TO Kal Winer and Noah Tatelbaum Winer, for critical reading and cheer leading.

TO Harriet Frank Tatelbaum, Milton Tatelbaum, and Harold Winer, for believing in me, even from the grave.

TO Michael Burke, Jean Sanborn, Christopher Fahy, Bill Roorbach, Joan Dye Gussow for careful reading and helpful comments.

TO Rob Shetterly, for lending me "A Woman Who Speaks Tree" for the cover.

TO Fred Ribeck and Lurelle Cheverie, for helping me design this book.

TO Colby College, for Humanities Grant and Media Services assistance.

TO Jim Fleming, for Friends of the Beeches.

TO Bro Adams, for making it possible, and necessary, to speak Tree.

TO my students, too many to name, for tugging these ideas out of me.

TO Al Gore, for inspiration.

Contents

Preface

This is the story of how trees saved me. How they guided me along the route to finding my root. And how I try to save them in return. Their wisdom is the core of this book, and my life stories are the growth rings.

I'm one of those baby-boomers who went to live a rural life in the 1970s. I still answer to the name of hippie, though I've also spent a career in college teaching while living this hard-earned organic life on the homestead we built in Maine. Daily conversations with trees show me that "being green" isn't just about saving the environment, but actually learning from it. Trees are the real teachers.

We live in a time when, ironically, planting trees is viewed as one solution to the damage we've done by removing trees. This book is a memoir with a mission. May the environmental crisis we face, and the call for human ingenuity, teach us to respect nature for the lessons it offers on how to live.

Study trees. Always look up. Always listen. Be small in their shadow. Walk tall like the moonlit stripes they lay across the road in winter. Bend in the wind. Bow to the ice. Sleep when it's cold, and blush with rising sap in early spring.

One could do worse than be a hugger of trees. Press the bark to your heart and feel the beat. Sap flows, pulse goes. Trade oxygen and carbon dioxide. Merge.

What is the difference between tree and me? I walk, I talk. Yet we both put down roots, produce seeds, seek the sun, drink water. I live in a shelter built with the aid of my opposable thumb. A tree is its own shelter. I have arms to wield a hoe and carry baskets of food from garden to kitchen. I cook, eat, wash my bowl. A tree is all arms, reaching for food and giving food, patient, yearning, generous, proud.

What is the difference between tree and me? Maple, birch, pine, oak, hemlock, all die. Me too. But I will not be lumber, or wooden bowls, or paper. I will be ash or worms, perhaps to make a flower grow. A tree is more useful to me than I to it. My living threatens its life. I can't help but take from it. All I can give in return is a voice to sing its praise.

There is no difference between tree and me. To study trees is to study me. We are trees, didn't anyone tell you? Trees that walk and talk. Trees with ambitions, and tools. We need to be careful how we hold that saw, lest we cut our own selves down.

Paper Scissors Rock

During the March thaw, finding high water flowing over the little stone bridge, I give up my walk and turn back toward home. Then I hear a chainsaw on the other side. I've vowed to protect this land, so I pick my way across the lip of the bridge on a line of exposed stones.

Following the noise, sure enough, just below the ledgy cliff that forms the farthest boundary, I find him. A guy with ear protectors, cutting everything on his side of the line. I squat behind a rotting log and look down at his yellow hardhat, the chainsaw slicing fir, cedar, pine. My trees are safe. Flapping orange ribbons distinctly mark the border at the top of the outcrop where I'm hidden. He's not trespassing, so at least I won't have to fly into a rage. But I feel so sad to be where primeval woods studded with hut-size boulders declare that some things can't be owned, now shaved clean right to the edge.

I know, I know—he needs to make a living. I have my work as teacher and writer. He has his truck, his chainsaw. Necessity drives us both, but where are the boundaries? Clear-cutting is a sharp *take-take-take*, yet I can't deny that my paper career depends on his work cutting pulp. But I need the wild. His relentless chainsaw makes me fierce and lonely, Cassandra in a flannel shirt crouching behind a blow-down.

I head away from the awful din, back to the bridge. Cassandra was a prophet whose curse was that no one believed her. She would not crouch. She would stand right up and tell the guy to leave as much as he took. He would take what he wanted just the same. Some things never change. I arrive at the bridge and carefully step along the line of stable rocks. Stop halfway across. Listen—rushing water drowns out the chainsaw sound!—and take another step, happy. A stone tips. I spiral down, grind my shin on a pointed rock as I pivot into the icy creek, an arm, an ear, the ends of my hair. Flannel sleeve soaked, heavy, pulls me under. My view is suddenly treetops. A voice says, "Uh-oh. Not good. Not good at all." The voice gives me something to grab onto. Somehow I scramble out of the flood and drag twisted hip along the trail. It happens so fast I'm home before I start to bawl.

Just missing the shinbone, a deep internal puncture that doesn't break the skin bleeds inside and turns black, purple, blue. The wound: shaped like a parenthesis (in which to insert a last happy thought—the sound of a rushing brook—and maybe to drown...

But I don't drown. The parenthesis opens but it doesn't close.

When nature is taken for money, who is hurt? The one who stops to listen. Not the one with ear protectors and chainsaw. The one saved by maple trees who say "uh-oh, not good" as the woman who loves them tumbles off the bridge. And do trees say "uh-oh, not good" when the guy starts up the saw? Do they mind being cut? The question haunts me. Who saves whom, and by what promises?

The old stone bridge was long abandoned by 1977, when Kal and I arrived here in Burkettville, Maine, a hamlet within the small town of Appleton, and parked a faded pink trailer on the edge of the wild. We hacked out a garden from witchgrass, milkweed, bramble, rock. We built a south-facing house to absorb the sun's heat, and cut wood for the cookstove by hand. We scarcely had time to explore the rest of the property, where the bridge marks a boundary between our busy home acres and an overgrown field at the back. Under the bridge flows a stream that drains water from the woods down to the marsh I like to call Biotica, and onward to the Medomak River, Muscongus Bay, the Atlantic Ocean, the clouds. The bridge is not a legal boundary. We "own" both sides. It's a spiritual border-crossing, and marks the distance between the zone of human enterprise and a place of magic.

Twenty acres was all we wanted. It's a long story, and I mean to tell it, about how we ended up with these seventy-five acres of cut-over woods at a bargain price, and even before that, what propelled us to drop out of nascent careers and follow the back-to-the-land path trod by our generation. The land was here before we found it, hilly woodland fretted with old logging trails, a twenty-acre marsh, and beyond the bridge, a ten-acre back field: extra, unsought, a mythic place removed from human presence.

Human absence is marked by corduroy ridges left at the last plowing over a century ago. They opened up the furrows, but never closed them. Maybe father died, or the oxen got sick, or they gave up and moved to town. The land passed out of the Sukeforth family and became, not something to nurture for generations, but a commodity called "acreage." Pines crept in. Loggers cut them off in the 1950s. That's why it was a bargain, this rugged land from which so much has been taken since the day the Sukeforths led the oxen back over the bridge and never returned to sow their corn. All human enterprise was silent by the time we came. Let the bridge demarcate a holy buffer: we will pay for this unexpected gift with our vigilance.

Most people would say a bridge epitomizes human enterprise. We found an old map with the back field circled and a pencilled note: "No rocks." Sukeforth and his sons paid with sweat labor so they could drive wagons across the stream and make use of their fertile hilltop. Only a couple of hippie dreamers could look at the big stones laid skillfully over the water in a low arch, the eight-foot–wide roadway covered with sod, and see it as a magic gateway to wilderness.

We soon discovered this mythic place was not our secret. Hunters know all about the field we thought we'd discovered. And what could I say when I spotted a blue tarp flapping on a half-built cabin just the other side of the property line? The back field is the remote edge of our land, and that makes it the closest to neighboring human presence. Holy to us, it was already a known place in which we were the newcomers.

Still, that heartfelt vow to protect it makes me do risky things like cross a flooded bridge to spy on a woodcutter. I already know rage does no good. In a recurring nightmare, I'm walking in the back field when I come upon a race-track. Dirt bikes roar past me in a clatter of tossed beer cans. Cheering spectators sit on bleachers scarfing hot dogs from a little shack with a flag on it. I flip into Madwoman, waving my arms—STOP!—WHAT ARE YOU DOING?—NO——while circling bikes throw dust in my face. At least they could have offered me a hot dog.

This is vintage Cassandra. Luckily, I wake up. But the nightmare has been fulfilled if you total all the changes we've seen around here. Logging, mining, gas pipelines, highways, superstores, yes, even race-tracks. What can one madwoman do?—*STOP! THE LAND IS ALL WE HAVE!*—No one hears.

Those treetops that pulled me from the flood remain etched on my vision. I suspect they colluded in getting me to cross the bridge. I heard the chainsaw, and had to go stand witness under a canopy of grief. The rushing brook soothed me with joy on my return. Then *whaap!*—the stone tips.

Nothing is permanent. That's the lesson. A bridge crosses both ways, with no place to stop and say let's keep things the way they were. Everything goes on changing. The lesson of the bridge throws the idea of preservation, of protection, upside-down into the flood. Who knows the just form of a place, unless they possess the eye of treetops?

Of course we believe our changes have improved the homestead we found overgrown by a century of neglect. A fallen cellarhole and two dug wells were all that remained of the old Sukeforth place, a huge lilac bush and sour rhubarb at the base of an old grapevine. But who says productivity and order restore this land to *what it should be*? Monarch butterflies preferred the milkweed we uprooted. Partridge and whippoorwills nesting in the empty cellarhole have since gone away. Porcupines, skunks, woodchucks, slugs, mice, are persecuted pests now. Pine saplings born to reach for the sky are yanked in favor of tomatoes and lettuce. "Sorry," I say when I do it, but does that make it okay?

We arrived intent on escaping the 1970s, the debt-driven consumer frenzy, loss of neighborly community, oil shortage and political scandals. If nothing is permanent, then why do identical problems continue to plague us? Kal and I came here to live like eighteenth-century settlers, but darned if the nineteenth and twentieth century didn't just go on flowing under the bridge. And now here it is, a brand-new century in which to cry out uselessly against modernity.

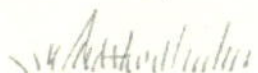

The bounded universe we call home—garden, brook, woods, marsh, and a hill of rock and oak—shouldn't be that hard to protect, we thought. Town is another story. For the original Abenaki, or Dawn People, who planted corn, beans, and squash in these upland valleys, then migrated to the coast to evade mosquitoes and enjoy lobsters, clams, and mussels all summer long, it was a seamless universe. Nowadays they'd be busted for trespass and unlawful taking of shellfish. "Ownership" arrived with Europeans in the 1760s, and the abundant harbor became a town named Cambden. Two centuries of fishing, shipping, textiles and leather, boom and bust, tourists and summer people, preceded the back-to-the-land migration of which we were a part.

Camden, in the 1970s, was a place of shady streets, clapboard houses with crooked shutters and overgrown honeysuckle. Downtown—hardware, grocery, clothing, five-and-ten, drug store, bank, post office, theater—the air was redolent with wood smoke, mildew, salt water, kerosene, fish. Like the Abenaki, we, too, headed for the coast after a long day planting the garden. Our shellfish ritual involved eating an honest lobster at a shack on the waterfront with a pot-bellied stove and oilcloth-covered tables. Sure, there were flower boxes, boutiques, waterfront estates. The smell of steak drifted along Bayview Street, and music throbbed from the pub. Sailboats in the harbor, camera-toting visitors, tea and scones at the bookshop. But underneath, Camden was just a rooted town where people lived in cozy proximity with nature.

Nearby Rockland, where it still felt like 1950 on Main Street, was where we ran errands when it was too muddy to work in the garden and too chilly in the trailer. We'd look for a public supper listed in the newspaper, and go eat baked beans and pie, often to benefit a hardship case in town. Old-fashioned community fed our illusion that Rockland would stay the way it was.

The way it was: lobstermen, sardine-packers, and lime-kiln workers lived on the waterfront. Next level, county and federal buildings, social services. Third tier, large homes with porches and shade trees. Back down near the smelly harbor, brick buildings with empty storefronts, except for a hardware store with nails sold by the pound, pharmacy with a black marble soda fountain, and purveyor of work clothes. A little art museum set back from the broken sidewalks of Main Street seemed out of place in the working-class town.

The museum's framed landscapes, by famous Maine artists, are the only thing that has stayed unchanged as more and more people followed our migration to midcoast Maine. And it's not as if we didn't make our own changes at home. Cross a rough lawn where there's no more pink trailer, past an array of solar electric panels. Pull a primitive latch string and the hand-made door pops open—that much has remained the same. But inside, no plywood floor with a dusty braided rug, no kerosene lamps. The oak floor is, by now, mellow with age, and the photovoltaic system installed in 1981 is already a dinosaur by today's standards. We've changed at the rate of our gradually accumulated savings, and rarely upgrade an upgrade. Make it a little better, then stop.

Changes in Camden and Rockland, though, never stop. Take a trip to the coast now, and witness what happened when credit-card giant MBNA took a liking to the abandoned mill in Camden, the "underutilized" Rockland waterfront, the gem of a museum, the picturesque hills and islands. We thought our backwoods was surely a place to escape change. But the newspaper tells us we live in the "sacrifice zone." We are a stockpile of natural and human resources. Besides the suit-and-tie telemarketing jobs in town, now any guy with a truck can join the boom, delivering lumber, gravel, rocks to the coast. Nature is the sacrifice in this game of Paper Scissors Rock. Paper money traded for a paper deed allows Scissors to decide what goes, what stays. Rock is scraped and shaped for buildings agleam with glass. Diesel power, hydraulic power, dynamite if you have to. Whatever it takes. Because it's ours. Because we can.

Poor old Cassandra. She warned her people that the Trojan horse was a dangerous trick. But they fell for it anyway, bringing on war and destruction. Do I, who need neither corporate nor construction job, have a right to warn that the new prosperity could spell our doom? Camden rejoiced when the dilapidated woolen mill was converted into a telemarketing center. Now it's already abandoned, to become condos with crisp awnings and perfect stone walls, but no jobs. Instead, a brand new credit-card center was built in Rockland on prime waterfront property. Then that center closed, too, leaving unemployment and a real estate market in shambles. Even MBNA went under, swallowed by the Bank of America like the rest of us.

Change keeps right on changing. Not even Cassandra can know

the just form of a place. The god Apollo tried to rape her, the most beautiful daughter of King Priam and Hecuba of Troy. She resisted, so he condemned her to prophesy the truth and have no one believe her. What is the truth, in this case? We're supposed to be delighted by all this upscale development, and I do love a certain café and the refurbished movie theater. But let the old virtues speak—thrift, modesty, caution with resources. All I know is we're destroying the Rock that sustains us. No one hears.

Rock is quiet. The quiet of after, as when all planes were grounded on September 11th, is not what I seek on this December day, crossing the bridge on snowshoes, down through pines and birches to stand among cattails in the frozen marsh. Here in Biotica I find the quiet of before, the original peace of any winter solstice. I come to hear life speak without lips, to read the familiar landscape like a prayer known by heart—silvery dead cedar trunks, stiff reeds, animal tracks. I'm following the buried stream, aiming for the deep center of the watershed where everything collects and continues seaward.

Solstice sun drops, and pale beams strike alders straight on. Our neighbors' rounded hill of rock left by the glacier casts a dark blue shadow. Ice and thaw have cracked the rock into square-edged blocks, wind and rain wrapped them in soil. A regal hemlock forest slopes up to tall white pines, crowned by an oak plateau. It is an unnamed heap. Unlike the World Trade towers, it cannot fall.

But name a thing—Map x, Lot y—and it becomes something to take. An alien *beep-beep-beep* alarms me, and I lift my hat to listen ...*beep-beep-beep-beep.....*, the sound a "sacrifice zone" makes. Roar of bulldozer, clang of chains, the rock-on-rock groan of boulders wrenched from their earthen lodge, the song of glacial action in fast-forward. The timeless quiet of before is lost as I wait, tensed, for the next fleet of rumbling trucks.

I have to go see. It's 3:30, and getting dark. I part shoulder-high reeds, grab alders to pull myself up to the road. Unstrap snowshoes, stow them behind a cedar tree, and walk toward the horrific sound. These gouged ruts will become brown rivers when it rains. Two trucks careen down the S-curves, headlights on. I face the other way to avoid watching huge shelves of quiet rock, bound in chains, worth thousands of dollars, leave the hill. They are the hill. The hill is leaving. The quiet of before is gone forever, here as in the world.

Unheard over the roaring trucks, I shout, "Leave those rocks where they belong!" Madwoman again. But who am I to say rocks "don't want" to be moved? Maybe they "like" being re-incarnated as the beautiful stone walls of a booming economy. Maybe they "hurt" underground, wedged against each other. Maybe this is liberation, leaving the hill for a new life in town. Washington, D.C. was built from granite quarried on Vinalhaven Island, across the bay from Rockland. What a life for an island rock, to house such power! And what a fate for my neighboring rocks to become the new wing of the art museum where visitors can admire landscapes that no longer exist.

Anyway, materials have to come from somewhere. I turn away from the receding trucks and head home in the dusk. My house is built from hemlock, spruce, pine, oak, birch, trees that thrive in this forest. Native cultures used deer hide and gut, bark, grasses, gourds. Where's the boundary between use and abuse? If you call a place "home," the boundary comes clear. And every place is home to someone.

"Dominion" does not mean lordship. The root of the word, *domus*, means home. If the rock-miners lived on the hill, they wouldn't be removing it piece by piece. Not so long ago, these coveted rocks were a nuisance. The Sukeforths and their oxen removed them to the edge of the back field. Stone walls said "home" in a language of human scale. A man could place rocks with such skill that his boundary walls remain even as his gravestone tilts to the earth. He hadn't the ability, or the time, to mine a hill of buried rocks and haul them to town.

Instead, he lived in its welcome shade, and called it "mine" for the riches it provided—wild life, wood lot, berry patch, medicine chest.

Nature is the abundant source of all our profit. Paper burns and Scissors melt, but the game of Paper Scissors Rock puts raw nature at the mercy of human invention. We must have mercy, then: use tools to extend a human hand in ways that don't hurt. The choice is ours: merciful, merciless; tool, weapon. But which is which? The stone tips. The unanswerable taunts me. *Shhhhh*...the wind in the cedars comforts me as I retrieve my snowshoes from their hiding place. It whispers what the Cassandra in me can't see. *Shhhh... Rock is. There's no before. There's no after. Stop halfway across the bridge. Listen to the stream...there's always more.*

Whaap! The stone tips. Nothing is permanent. Only the moment. Stay here. Now. Here. Now.

All winter long we lived with what I've come to call rock music. Might as well dance to it. Grief and fury are not good for us, and the world is full of problems reflected in this place. The rockers are quiet this June day. Walking along the road with Kal, past the gone woods where we once listened for the trilling of a hermit thrush, we hear only silence. Kal turns back at the rockers' rough driveway, and I decide to climb alone. I know I'm trespassing, but I have to see for myself.

The road threads through what's left of noble oaks. At each curve of the S, slabs await transport. Yanked stumps lie upside-down on the banks. Empty oil cans, styrofoam cups, greasy rags. Higher and higher, the hill puts a limit on the strength of my legs. I am not a diesel-eating Kubota. And not even a madwoman now, but someone making her way to a funeral. Warily I move past an orange backhoe with its fierce head bowed to the ground, and reach the baked plateau.

When Thoreau approached the untouched peak of Mt. Katahdin, the wind warned him back to where nature is kind—"Why came ye here before your time?" The voice I hear in these disturbed woods is not a threat but a sigh of fatigue. I follow the alley cut through a vast field of broken rock, staggering back when I come to a sheer rock face, the earth's gaping wound. I let loose a wail—You made me who I am—Who will I be without you?—

Why came ye here...? I came because I love you. I came to bear witness. *Go back to where nature is kind. Back to your root, the girl who loved trees without bitterness.* But what do I do with my grief? *Go back. Love is the root. From there, speak.*

Tears spatter the rock as I clamber onto a smooth slab among the thousands here, scalding my bare legs. No color but grey and brown. Cobalt sky. No birds. I'm looking straight into the eye of earth. Nothing I can do but sit here breathing. Listen to a distant song sparrow, lovely and soothing.

Something moves, far off among the stockpiles. It looks like a bird stuck between the rocks, with green wings fluttering wanly. I watch from this distance, afraid to cross the desert waste. It's not a bird. Shade my eyes against the glare. Focus. It's a lone sapling, trying to fly away with its two leaves flapping in the hot wind. A little moose maple, having the last word for the wild. *Cherishh... YESSSSSS... cherishhh...*

Abandoned Houses, Empty Jars

It's New Year's Eve, and I'm spending the last few hours of 1972 listening to Route 25, trucks going by beyond the pine trees that shelter the back of my house on Lake Shore Drive. New Hampshire State Route 25 coming from the west traces Lake Winnipesaukee until it comes to the blinking-yellow-light hamlet of Center Harbor, then continues northeast toward Moultonboro, Tamworth, West Ossipee. That's the only road to anywhere else, all the way to Maine and the sea.

It's so quiet tonight, I can hear big rigs climbing the far-off hill out of Meredith, speeding along the lake and downshifting at the blinking light. In the silence between trucks, I get an eerie feeling, as if my life has always been heading for this yellow house. Being 25 myself, and the new English professor at tiny Belknap College, I'm desperate to stake out some privacy. I trust this house hidden behind two huge willows to keep me safe, and I believe in the road that brought me here. My red Volkswagen sailed through the dark along Lake Shore Drive last August like the pointer on a Ouija board. I even turned the headlights off and let go of the wheel, and we drove in and out of tree-shadows cast on the pavement by the summer moon.

No house in sight, the car halted on a grassy shoulder, stopped by two willows draped to the ground. *Whhooohh, shhuuuhh...,* they beckoned me across the dewy grass. I nearly tripped over a hand-lettered sign—FOR SALE. Parting their long tresses, *Whhooohh, shhaahh...*, the willows waved me toward the door. I pressed my nose to the glass, fell in love with the wide pine floor. Is that a woodstove? Moonlight shone blue-white through the slats of a blind.

Next day, at the doorstep again with the elderly owner, I glanced up into the willows swaying and winking in morning sun, *Shhhhhh... whfffff....* Eva looked deep in my eyes, seeming to know something about me. She flicked her cigarette butt into the unkempt grass.

"'T'ain't much," she declared, turning the big Alice-in-Wonderland door knob, keyhole gaping like a mouth that speaks, no key. The musty cottage was not as it seemed last night. Floor not pine but linoleum patterned like wood. No woodstove but a kerosene heater. Turquoise walls with peeling paint, stained ceiling. "Oh, I like this room," I exclaimed as we crunched over the cracked linoleum tiles of the big country kitchen. My rocking chair could go right here, next to the round-edged refrigerator. A braided rug over the awful floor. Bread baking in the oven. Yes. Home.

"That stove burns kerosene for heat, on the end here, and the oven's electric. 'T'was very modern in my day! Did all my cannin' here. Big garden out back. Chickens, too." She lit up another cigarette while I opened a pantry cupboard filled with spiderwebs. "I can't really buy a house just yet," I admitted, and stooped by the front window to look up into the dazzling willows.

"You up to the college?" she asked, taking a drag of her cigarette. I nodded. She must think I make a bundle. She doesn't know I got this job by the skin of my teeth, even paying my own way to the interview. You take what you can get when there's a glut of new Ph.D.'s and no job openings.

"It's my son Irad wants me to sell the place. I'm next door with him now."

"Is there a cellar?" I asked, walking through the dusty living room toward the bedroom in back.

"Oh, yes, but I can't make it down the ladder no more. Trap door's here, right next to the bed." Imagine rolling out of bed and down the hatch like Alice. Eva was peering out the back window at a collapsed henhouse and two big pear trees. "Them pears is hard ones, good for cannin'." She studied my face as if seeing her young self. My communion with the trees pleased her. "You seem to love it," she squinted, smoke coiling toward one eye. I was already scattering feed for my fantasy hens. "I don't have to sell it right now. I'll rent it to you."

I knew I was home. You learn what home is when you're living in an alien place like Southern California, in a town where all the orange groves have been bulldozed for subdivisions, and your college sweetheart (husband, for now) has his first teaching job while you write your dissertation in a ticky-tacky house with a desert cooler cranking away on the roof. Autumn meant dry heat, high winds, terrifying forest fires. I took walks along hot streets with pretty Spanish names, heading toward the mountains that rimmed the valley town, invisible in the smog. I tried to ignore the abominable pastel stucco houses with cactus gardens in the yards. One day, I came to a scruffy driveway that interrupted all that neat pebble mulch. It disappeared between two houses and I followed.

At the end of the lane, a cluster of overgrown grapefruit trees, a battered shed, and a house, call it a shack. A loaded persimmon tree was plopping deep orange fruits onto the decaying roof. The door tilted on one hinge. Broken windows, rotted floor, bedspring, rusty basin. Here was a house, a real house, hidden behind the stage-set suburbia. Here was land that brought forth food. It was easy to imagine chickens scratching in the dust, an egg basket on the kitchen counter, and jars of persimmon jam. Reluctantly I turned away from my vision. Home is a place that feeds you, a shelter growing out of the land like a tree. Home is a place you have to find alone.

And now I'm alone, and I found it here at the yellow house.

It's close to midnight on this New Year's Eve, and I haven't heard a truck go by for quite some time. The howling wind shakes the windowpanes. The kerosene burner grumbles with each gust, and the kettle settles into a slow simmer. There's nothing to do at night in Center Harbor except rock by the stove with your feet on a braided rug.

The TV glows blue in Eva's window every evening, and they go to bed early. Get up early, too. I know, because a couple weeks ago, when we had our first blizzard, I was digging my way out for an 8 o'clock class. Okay, that's not completely true. I was digging out the Dean of Students. Kal is a friend, and I tried all semester to get him to come for supper. He lives thirty miles from here, and he's a home-body like me. Wants to sleep in his own bed. Not that I was inviting him to sleep in mine. But that's what happened, because of a blizzard.

He called from the college and said it's too stormy to head for Gilmanton, and can he come over? He arrives with his emergency toothbrush and underwear in a brown grocery bag. He paces back and forth on this braided rug as the snow mounds deeper outside. He just can't give himself up to being here, no matter how much I ply him with hot chili and cornbread. Finally the storm lets up some, and he decides to try for home, which pisses me off because I want company. He says goodnight, and backs out of the driveway—right into a snow-bank, ha ha. Now he'll stay for sure. But no. He comes in, stomping snow off his boots, to call AAA. The tow guy can't help because he has to babysit, so Kal's stuck here. What is he worried about? It's not like anyone from the college ever comes this far down the road, to see his distinctive old black Volvo in my driveway. Anyway, it's buried now.

In the morning, we're digging him out before it's light. He's very anxious to leave. We're both new at the college, and maybe he has a point, that we should be more discreet. But I mean, who's looking? The whole village is asleep under new snow. We dig, and rock his car, and push, and the tires race, and we're falling down laughing. Finally, just at dawn, a light goes on next door at Eva's. I see her smoking and watching us from the window that overlooks our parallel driveways, as her son Irad holds back the curtain. They watch us get Kal unstuck, watch him drive off. Watch me discover problems of my own. My VW is parked in the ramshackle garage between our two houses, with snow drifted up against the outward-opening door. Snowdrifts are dense, I soon learn, like a mass of tiny beebees. The gallant Irad appears in parka and storm-pack boots, and we dig the garage door free in time for my early class. That's the way of Yankee neighbors, I know now. They peek through their windows and evaluate, and once you prove you can cut it, they show up to lend a hand. But one corollary is, always help a solitary female before an able-bodied male, especially if he just spent the night with your tenant. Maybe Kal was right about discretion. The willows don't hide everything.

The heck with what Eva and Irad think. I wish stay-at-home Kal were here tonight. I could have gone to his house for New Year's Eve, but I'm just as set in my ways. He's happy living in an old farmhouse with his sister and brother-in-law while he builds a cabin in their woods. They're kind of a commune. Another man lives there in a tipi. I don't see how I fit in. I'd rather sit in my yellow house and dream about that old persimmon shack. I keep telling myself it was beyond repair, and yet I saw those chickens pecking, those jars of jam. I know abandoned houses need to be lived in. Empty jars need to be filled.

I lift a slat of the Venetian blind and peer at the night. It's not snowing, only blowing, and the road looks clear except for a spine of ice. I layer on scarf and parka, pull the glass door closed behind me. The bare willows whoosh and whip in the moonlight. Eva's house is all dark.

Lake Winnipesaukee—"sigh of the Great Spirit"—calls me to the one remaining open field that borders its edge, when, *HORrrrrrrr.....WOOoooooooo,* a dead elm guarding a wreck of a house stops me in my tracks. Eva told me the house lodged summer guests back when Center Harbor was a tourist haven. She said they came up the lake by steamboat from the railway in Laconia. I call the house haunted because I imagine them rocking on the porch and looking at the lake, having just eaten a wonderful country dinner of fresh chicken and biscuits and garden vegetables, and now the house is a shell and the guests are skeletons and the elm tree that shaded them is dead. But it's not really haunted. It's just a collapsed building, way beyond repair, even in fantasy. It's a shape, is all. Gable roof, front porch, door frames. I'm curious to see if there are any of those blue Mason jars, but so far I don't have the nerve to get close.

The house is a blackness, a whiteness, empty and lonely. It glowers in the overgrown yard. Doesn't like what's become of it. Doesn't like the paved road. Doesn't like the trees that block the view. Doesn't like the rotted floorboards, chipped basins, jars filled with cobwebs. It's hungry. It wants to provide. It wants the front porch sheltered under a canopy of elm. Wants to hear the screen door slam, the wicker rocker squeak. It wants... *GRRRNNNnnn... KRAAAK ...... THMPppm!* A dead elm branch crashes from the heights and lands smack at my feet. Bounces once for emphasis, and lies still.

I turn and flee to my yellow haven, practically skating along the ice-bone in the road, too scared to cry, toward the lighted window. Rattle the glass door closed. Pull the blinds. No Kal here tonight to keep the home fire burning. No one to greet me but my life. I wrap it around me like a quilt, and toast 1973 with a cup of cocoa—*To Life!*

Well, I sure am a recluse now, sitting in my same old rocker but at Kal's cabin in the woods this cold morning. One year has passed since that night spent listening to distant trucks ring in the first new year as driver of my own life.

What happened was, Sara and Jerry wanted Kal out of the farmhouse by winter, so I moved to Gilmanton to help finish this cabin. We'll all share the taxes and the garden. There's a phone in the barn.

But there are rules. Jerry says don't knock on the door before noon even if I need to fill the water jugs. Abe the tipi man does his turn at the laundromat and stuffs hot clothes into the bag, but it's too bourgeois to complain about rumpled duds. Sara says park the cars where they can't be seen from the farmhouse.

We walk across a hay field to get to this one-room house surrounded by pines. It shouldn't really have taken Kal so long to build what we call "the woods house," nor us two so many weekends to finish. But plastic that luffs on the rough window openings and a latchless door can defeat a dean and professor. A former dean and professor, I should say.

Yes, the Trustees pulled the plug on Belknap College in the fall, just after tuition was collected, of course. Instead of a needy college with its burdensome payroll, they preferred prime real estate—brick mansion on rolling hillside with White Mountain view. And me, I was Alice in a wonderland of my own making. "They won't do that," I kept repeating at faculty meetings, naïve new professor of English tucked into the branches of her favorite tree reading a book of fantasy. "They'll never close us down." But they did, and we graduated our last class in December, in the village church. As smiling Trustees filed past a pew of professors, I glared from under my gold-tasselled mortarboard. You would think a divorce, a glutted market for doctors of philosophy, a small-potatoes first job would have prepared me for life's disappointments. You'd think the Vietnam War or Watergate would have shattered my faith, or the oil embargo that pushed my heating bill out of reach. It took the Trustees' betrayal to open my eyes. Not only did I have to leave the house of willows; I'm through with the halls of ivy, too.

So we two unemployed academics struggled to get the woods house closed in "before the snow flies," consulting carpentry books at every turn. No books told us how to cross a field in a stiff wind while carrying big sheets of window glass between us without getting blown away. We twitched the wide panes this way and that down the narrow path. Caulked and tapped them in place just as snow flew. Too late for improvements. Winter came down on us and we live here now. At least no more billowing plastic keeps us awake. The outward-opening door latches with a block of wood from the outside, a hook and eye from the inside. That will have to do.

After the crashing elm branch scared me half to death last New Year's Eve, the half of me that lived did enjoy adventures heading east on Route 25. Nights, my car and I would pull out under a dome of stars, classical music on WQXR from New York City. Drive and drive through sleeping villages lined with black trees. Stop at a diner in Madison, eat pie with the truckers. Drive home to sleep. Winter days, drive along the Kancamagus Highway, gasping at Mt. Washington's snowy flanks. Eat bread and cheese, and watch the Swift River tossing water and ice. Summer, climb Mt. Chocorua with its pointed rocky top, blueberries partway down, stop to nibble. Pitch a tent at the base. Cook rice over campfire. Autumn, drive all the way east to Maine, gather rose-hips at Ogunquit.

A year of freedom. And then Alice tumbled down the hole, watching her tree house get smaller and smaller. Eva offered me the yellow house for cheap. She wanted someone who would fill the cellar with jars of pickles, tend the pear trees out back, and wear a path to the chicken shed. But without my teaching job, I couldn't keep up with the rent anymore, or even the heating bill. I loved the house, but was swept away by the scattering denizens of a defunct college. As I drove off for the last time, I saw Eva and the willows waving good-bye in my rear-view mirror. I followed Jerry's blue pick-up with the rocking chair tied on top. Next stop, Gilmanton, and another New Year, 1974.

The half of me that lived wants roots. One adventure on Route 25 turned me into a country woman who can't just go wherever the job market sends her. Home is a place you choose. Even now and even though I'm living at Kal's, I cling to that old belief in the rightness of the road. On that trip, a cottonwood towering over spring fields drew me to a dirt driveway in Tuftonboro, on the east side of Winnipesaukee. Not having learned my lesson from the life-or-limb elm, I got out under a high canopy of quivering new leaves. The ancient tree floated soft catkins from the heights of its corrugated trunk onto a cluster of tumbledown sheds, an abandoned farmhouse with happy ghosts.

I crossed the patchy grass to the porch steps. Rotten floorboards sagged under the first living weight they'd felt in a long time. Pressed my nose to the rippled glass. The sun through quaking leaves sparkled on a table loaded with Mason jars. I had to have them! Shook the locked door. Peeked again. Who washed these jars so long ago, preparing to can grape jelly from that gnarled vine climbing the shed wall? I felt her eyes on me, enchanting me with her song. *Capture the glory of the grape, let it enter the dark tunnel of your mouth and give you life on its way to death. Fill your cellar with summer's light.*

I had no cellar to call my own, no garden yet. I turned to go. But the rustling cottonwood urged me to take another look through the glass. A woman at the black iron sink with her hands in soapy water. Did she come all this way from the persimmon shack in Southern California, to wash these jars and pluck grapes from the vine?

I stepped back from the window, nearly tripped over a carton of empty jars on the stoop. Take them? I peeked again, looking for guidance. A ribbon laid out along the windowsill, cross-stitched with silver thread, winked at me in the filtered sunlight. "L-O-V-E G-O-D." I craned up at the cottonwood. Me? *Yesssssss.* I loaded the box of jars into the red VW and drove off, blessed with quarts and pints to start the life I saw inside that kitchen—my chosen life.

The road just keeps giving you the next thing. Like this woods house, which lacks that haunted feel. It's young. Fragrant blond lumber, clear new glass. We'll plant a garden, and fill those jars. But this is no abandoned house for me to breathe life into. This is Kal's place. He was headed here, and when I fell off my perch, I landed in his nest.

This morning we awoke to frost-ferns on the windows, twenty

below zero outside. Kal left before dawn for the factory where he took a job when the college closed. We don't light the kerosene lamp in the day, so I'm rocking in the dark with hands tucked under legs. The green-and-cream cookstove gobbles a mouthful of wood every hour, but it's no match for this cold. I'm getting scared as the temperature slides back with every log I shove in. A grim light seeps through iced windows. I can't see the pines and they can't see me. I feel like an abandoned house myself, a jar with nothing inside.

The woodbox needs filling, so I pull on my boots to go out to the woodpile. Chop wood, carry water, these are my jobs while Kal's operating a lathe for minimum wage. I push on the door. Push...on the door. The door...? No! Kal forgot, and turned the block on the outside that keeps it closed. I'm trapped in here!

Stumble back to the rocking chair. Cry and scream. No one can hear. What happened to my life? Oh, where do I even start to put the pieces back together?

My furious rocking inches the chair closer to the kindling box behind the stove. I see a newspaper sticking out between wood scraps. A boldface advertisement grabs my attention. START HERE, it suggests. And like Alice with her "eat me" mushroom, I ingest these words and suddenly I'm bigger. I can see a future up ahead, if I just start here. Where else? This is the road. There is no other.

A Palindrome Journey

If ever there was a palindrome journey, it has to be the trip from New Hampshire to West Virginia (and back) that Kal and I began in September. Even now in late November with a lonely Thanksgiving staring us in the face, no home, no jobs, no prospects, I still don't know where we're going. We started 1974 living together in Kal's cabin in the woods, behind the sagging old Cape his sister Sara and her husband Jerry bought in Gilmanton. Abe, the tipi guy who lived in another part of the woods, had left, so when I entered the scene last winter, the commune grew from three to four, and four became two and two with a hay field in between.

Slowly the rough cabin became our home. Rug and chair, tea kettle, high stool by the long west window for contemplating beech trees the other side of a stone wall. Pines on our side, deep and soft, with stumps and a bench in the sunny clearing. Culture the yogurt, soak the beans, sweep the floor. Punch down the cracked-wheat bread, chop wood, carry jugs of water from Sara's across the field. Empty the dirty water bucket outside on the pine needles. Trim the wick and light the lamp.

The phone in the barn kept the world at bay. If someone heard the ring, and someone answered, a message might or might not be scratched on the back of a seed packet with a dull pencil. In the optimism of spring, we planted a serious food garden—squash, corn, beans, potatoes, carrots, onions, tomatoes, and way too many rutabagas—without a thought about how to preserve the harvest, or how we'd divvy it up. We bickered about who's supposed to prune the tomatoes how, who planted green beans on top of the beet row because who didn't write what on the garden map. We all loved the field of waving Timothy grass, black-eyed Susans, and purple vetch, and I voted to leave it growing wild. But a hay field is for hay, it seems, and when I heard the old tractor going 'round and 'round, I got the message. This may be your home, but it is not your place. Kal and I stayed until harvest, stored our share of rutabagas and jars of tomatoes in the back room of the farmhouse where they won't freeze, and in September we left for West Virginia in the Volkswagen: WVVW.

WVVW is a palindrome. Those initials might have told us something about how a journey encounters obstacles and slides back through all the same places in reverse. You slip off course a little at a time and slowly the palindrome becomes a learning curve, and you move on. What did we know? Certainly not that we'd be sitting here in a tacky motel room watching plastic curtains sway in the cold draft. If I trace this idealistic story—the dream of life on the land and in community—will I ever understand the journey that nourishes our generation even though it bruises us with disappointment? WVVW. I pray this motel is the final low point of the last W. Maybe from here there's only that one last upward stroke that will bring us home. Wherever that is.

WVVW is not only a palindrome, but a graphic depiction of the rugged Appalachian landscape we traversed looking for a small farm with house intact for $3000, just like *The Mother Earth News* promised. Picture our red beetle chugging along curvy roads past farms and rivers, in the shadow of steep hills whose crowded trees don't speak to me. Inside the car crammed with camping gear, two hippies in flight from civilization, in search of paradise. We are a palindrome-in-motion as we start each day with more and more hope, driving up rocky hollers to look at washed-out land and ramshackle huts where our fellow back-to-the-landers have settled with their naked children, no front door, pigs in the yard, tumbledown outhouse, the only sign of civilization a wad of food stamps on the cluttered kitchen table. And each evening, with less and less hope, we roll back down to a campsite in the valley, passing nice little white farms on "bottomland," rich by Appalachian standards, not the $3000 kind. Next morning, break camp, follow a mystical instinct sparked by some promising town name on the map, like Five Forks, where we actually do find a place that seems possible. Old hickory trees nicely shade a house and cellarhouse, which we learn is a root cellar built around a spring that keeps things cold, topped with a storage building. Five Forks, West Virginia—sounds like an address, could be home. Until we see rats in the cellarhouse and wonder what else we haven't noticed.

Despondent nights in our tent after a supper of rice cooked in a charred pot, the only entertainment being the campfire of wood we scrounge from empty campsites, or the thrill of finding something usable in the trash barrel. Morning, back on the tar roads, no more driving up hollers, no way will we live like that. In Spencer, we find a co-op store with its familiar smell of whole-wheat flour, Dr. Bronner's All-One Peppermint Soap, incense. Long-haired men, long-skirted women, dirty babies, dogs. And an ad for a house with "free gas." We go. Nice house, greenhouse, good windows, but what is "free gas"?

"Oh, it's a pretty good set-up," the seller remarks, thumbing through some catalogues to show us the windmill he almost spent a fortune on until he agreed to sign the government deal. "There's not all that much wind here anyway," he says, combing through his tousled hair with dirty fingers. "Too many hills." The house is way too hot inside with a gas furnace rumbling even though it's warm outside and the windows are open. He leads us out to show us the greenhouse, also heated with gas.

"You sell the rights to the natural gas under your property," he explains. "No biggie. You get to tap the line and use as much as you want. Why not? It's free! Free-ee! Hahahahaha." He knows he's pulling our Yankee chain. Kal mutters something about nothing free is free. "We do what we can," the guy asserts. "You will, too."

We'd chosen West Virginia because of the milder climate, the four seasons, but it does appear that life is not any easier than in New Hampshire. Harder, in fact, with ungenerous soil and rugged terrain. But as we drive away from Free Gas, we agree that nothing worthwhile is easy. Back at the Spencer co-op, we meet a few other back-to-the-landers who seem none too happy.

"Self-sufficiency!" snorts a woman who sees me leafing through an issue of *The Mother Earth News*. Her partner watches Kal fill a bottle with soybean oil from the spigot of a white bucket. "See? Ya gotta have money."

"What kind of work do you do for money?" I ask him as I scoop brown rice into a paper bag, and he says, "Coal."

Kal a coal-miner? No way. "Let's get the hell out of here," I whisper as we wait to pay for our food. The looming hills are suffocating, black with stunted trees. There's no radio reception. The hippies we're meeting either work as miners or play banjo and harmonica all day instead of chopping wood and gardening. Okay, so we're Yankee hippies.

"Let's try one more place," says Kal. "I don't know where else we can go. We can't go back." I have to go back, I'm thinking. Have to. But we're a couple now, and the VW is taking us west, an eager beetle leading once again into the unknown.

In the falling dusk, we spot a weathered old house with a truck up on blocks in the front yard. We knock. Door opens to the smell of canned green beans. Man in a white undershirt asks us in. He and his wife are about to sit down at a rickety kitchen table.

"You et?" he asks. "S'down." He heaps steaming food on two plates, green beans, succotash, squash, mounds of mashed potatoes, hot biscuits, a slab of home-cured ham. "Y'ain't poor if you got land," he declares. "I pity those folks in town, always grubbin' for a dime."

Once our plates are bare, the wife says, "Come see our cellar-house." We step out into the balmy fall evening, cross the yard to a little building with a stone foundation. An old door creaks open and we enter the musty cellar. No rats. Only bins of root crops all stored away for the coming winter, rows of canned goods, hanging hams. Bottles of milk sitting in a spring that runs down off the hill. This is the very life we're aiming for, except they learned the ways of foraging and farming from their elders and we haven't got a clue.

"We'll show you ever'thing we know," the man promises. "Don't you give up. Y'ain't poor long's yer back holds out."

Next morning, hope re-kindled, we follow instinct and not a map. We pass a sign that points up a rugged hollow. Sign says "Replete." The VW takes the turn and climbs in second gear up a winding trail of jagged rocks, switchbacks, ruts. "Replete"—the very name foreshadows fulfillment of the dream, at last! The bug crawls up the deserted road to heaven, in first gear now, carrying us to our destiny.

Replete, West Virginia: three shacks, twenty barking dogs, one broken-down 1940s truck, and some kids playing with sticks held like guns. They shoot us. We die.

From the perspective of this awful motel room so many miles from West Virginia, I can see that the journey of our generation begins somewhere, everywhere, nowhere. Maybe mine began in New Hampshire with the brown rice I ordered in bulk from a co-op in the corner of someone's kitchen, where lentils stuck to spilled honey tracked all over the floor. We are bound together in search of a dream where we all dip into the same sack and feed each other. And I still hold that dream, in spite of the starvation and isolation Replete had to offer, and the other bends in the road that keep bringing us from nowhere to nowhere else.

How we all came to repossess the connection to whole food, after urban or suburban name-brand childhoods—how we're dancing along in bare feet and colorful Pakistani shirts, following a road that began in the '50s with Ike and American flags and Scouts, and into the chaotic '60s—is a map of many contours, each of us travelling alone but moved by the pulse of a generation. Our generation's brand would be Erewhon, the company name emblazoned on all those whole foods at the little co-op where we gathered once a month for the breakdown of big bags into small, the many from the one. Erewhon is meant to spell "nowhere" backwards, the name Samuel Butler gave to his satirical and unlocatable utopia. Even here in the limbo of this motel, we manage to locate ourselves by eating plain food bought in brown bags, cooked on a gas burner in thrift-store pots, eaten with chopsticks from a wooden bowl.

Each in our own way, we are going in reverse to a backwards nowhere that probably doesn't exist. We tried the commune thing with Sara and Jerry, and suffered the collapse of that collective dream. We still trust our instinct, even though it turns out Replete was the pit, not the tip. The lesson is, get used to being toppled upside-down. Get used to going back. That day, we managed to turn the VW around on the parched grass with dogs lunging at the tires from both sides, and descended to seek new ground. Not back. Onward. The nowhere we're looking for must exist somewhere. But where? Erehw?

Once you hit Replete, where else can you go? Kentucky. And we do a very un-Yankee thing. We actually knock on Wendell Berry's door. It's not like we have a phone to call him from. We're sleeping in the Volkswagen, and we're down to the last few cups of rice, the bottom of the powdered milk box. It's late October, and we have no place else to go. We knock. No one home. Yankee enough not to look around on our own, at least. Next day, knock again on the farmhouse door that faces a steep field and, through a fringe of oaks, the glinting Kentucky River below. Wendell is a poet and farmer, a sage to us back-to-the-landers. He pulls open the door and stares blankly at this young couple, one bearded, one bandanna'd, as he's probably stared at other knocking couples before us. His face looks grim in the shadow of the front porch, and he pushes back his cap to scratch his head. He glances from one to the other, waiting for us to state our business.

"We're looking for a place to live on the land, like you," I mumble lamely. "We were wondering...if...um...you know of any farms for sale?"

Somewhat grudgingly he says, "Come on down to the barn with me while I doctor a sick horse." He pulls his cap low over his eyes, and strides downhill toward the river without looking back at us. We grin at each other and follow the X of his suspenders across the road and into the dark barn.

"Whoa, girl," he murmurs when the horse twitches her head up and flips her mane. He's quick and gentle with the ailing horse, and just as quick and gentle with us.

"We want to do what you're doing," says Kal, "you know...farming the home place."

"But this is not your home," he replies, not unkindly. "Where you from?"

"We were from New Hampshire. But we thought Kentucky might be..."

"We read in *The Mother Earth News* that West Virginia and Kentucky are good for what we want to do. Small farm, small house, you know," I elaborate.

"Go back and settle where you come from. That's what I did," says Wendell, who took up farming on fields his grandfather mowed with a team of horses, in a town that knows him without reading his books. The doctor's good medicine stings a bit, but we don't whinny. He hands me a carrot to feed the horse, and gives a little salute as he watches us troop back across the field to the VW.

Back home? Maybe for Wendell that was easy, but we are the Erewhon generation. We are from nowhere. We decide to try his prescription, though, and head north and east to Rochester, New York, my home town. Anything but New Hampshire, says Kal, who's still hurt by the collapse of the Gilmanton dream. We stay with my parents, and spend short November days looking at old farmhouses in the southern tier around Bath. One, with peeling paint and a bay window that overlooks a valley famous for "muckland" onions, distant hills planted to vineyards, almost makes the grade, but where would we work if we have to? Mom and Dad don't know what to make of their daughter the Ph.D. with her long dress and boots and short-cropped hair, and her bearded boyfriend. Should they share the guest room? Is she really "a god-damn fool," as Dad whispers to Mom?

Perhaps she is. Rochester roots don't hold us, and the road keeps rolling back toward New Hampshire. The minute we cross the border, the lavender blush of birch treetops on granite hills says "home" to me. Kal feels at home, too, as long as we stay on the west side of the state. So we stop in Keene, where we share a dingy rented room with another looking-for-land guy named Tim. But the road beckons east, the familiar Concord area calls our name. And then a little further east to Epsom, to this run-down motel with a thermostat in a locked box on the wall, set at 60 degrees. Thanksgiving will be mashed rutabagas and stewed tomatoes, which we'll go pick up from our stash in nearby Gilmanton while Sara and Jerry are meditating at the ashram. The string reeled out a piece just long enough to get us to Kentucky before it began to wind us slowly back, in despair, to where we began with high hopes. Now we live on a traffic circle with sulfur floodlights and a view of McDonald's Golden Arch. One sheltering pine keeps headlights from shining in, and reminds us of our home in the pine woods where this journey began. The future we envisioned in that place is already past. Living by kerosene light, by mice in the ceiling and cold air filtering up through the floor. By clothes hanging from nails on the wall, everything in the open, mugs and bowls on shelves made of rough boards. A portable toilet right in the one room with us, which sealed our intimacy. We've still got the intimacy, so I guess we came away with what really counts.

In fact, the portable toilet was what landed us, by this very long route, here at the Epsom Motel. Because the problem was, where do you dump it? The bottom of the toilet was removable, and clasped shut like a suitcase. Kal toted our waste across the field when Sara and Jerry were at the ashram, and flushed it down their toilet in two or three gulps. Big hullabaloo one Sunday when the toilet clogged, and we already sensed they didn't want us dumping there, and they were due home soon, too soon. Plunging and mopping and opening windows, fast, really fast. Rushed out of there with empty shitcase like thieves in the night.

Sara and Jerry were not pleased. Who could blame them? They went to the ashram to cleanse their soul, while back home we were unloading shit into their toilet. We tried to make amends by digging a hole for an outhouse next to our cabin. Luxury! And no loss of intimacy because in a one-room house there's no place to escape. Except the pine woods, which happily accommodate one and all with a cool sigh of welcome.

My heart breaks when I remember how the soft path weaves between dark trunks toward the brilliant light of the hay field. A big rock in the middle of the field, like the navel on a belly of grass, was a meditation seat, the sky a blue dome over all. Look one way, and see the trail to Kal's woods house. Look the other, and it's the old white farm, the driveway, Loon Pond Road leading out and away. What held us together, what broke us apart, was meditation. We're all in exile, learning to breathe and chant, learning that *Om* is home. We tried to simplify, to unify, but instead we complicated our commune with judgment, expectation, disappointment.

As soon as Sara and Jerry had a baby on the way, our fragile two-and-two dynamics broke down. Their nesting instinct kicked in, and they wanted to be a family of three. We two sat in our lamp-lit house, cultivating the *Mother Earth News* dream of a small farm at the end of a long driveway where an old couple would be rocking on the porch and wondering what to do with the place they'd devoted their lives to. We'd tool up in our red Volkswagen, all beaming and young, life-savings in hand. By Thanksgiving, we'd be in.

But here it is, Thanksgiving, and we're living miserably close to Gilmanton, without the nerve to address what hurt so bad before Tulsi was born. We had accepted the break-up as an opportunity to improve on the dream. We'd find a better house, or build one, plant a wiser garden. Maybe we'd even get married and have a child. But the way it happened was that one hot night last summer, before we had a chance to announce our decision to leave, full-bellied Sara came floating down the pine-needle path barefoot and told us we had to go.

Years after Sara and Jerry sold the farm, we took our boy back to see Gilmanton. By that time, we were a family of two families, and better friends than when we tried to make a commune together. We'd have been seven at the old butcher table by the kitchen window, with their Tulsi and Bodhi, our Noah. But a new owner answered our knock, and soon just we three were walking hand-in-hand across the hay field on a light crust of snow.

Noah loved the story of the woods house Dad built, but he didn't believe it was real until we came down through the pine trunks and saw it, empty and abandoned. We turned the block that still holds the door shut from the outside. It smelled cold inside, like creosote and dust. There was a stain on the floor the shape of the portable toilet. One empty Mason jar on the kitchen shelf. Kal made this cabin spring up in a time of dreaming, and here it still was, the starting-point of our palindrome journey. The last time we'd turned the block on the hand-made door, in September 1974, the unborn Noah hovered in the future, perhaps overseeing our move from the Epsom Motel to a rented house with a garden plot. From there, we ventured out and back for two more years, until the pine-green hills of Maine guided us to our home. In April 1977, Maine became the center of our next journey, not out and back this time, but down and down, growing a root strong enough to nurture a child, deep enough that we believe we'll grow old and die here.

The Don't-Know Dream

A roof is a good place to see ourselves the way trees do. I hope they're enjoying the comedy of two inept and anxious carpenters putting up an aluminum roof. From my perch on this ladder wedged between two bare rafters, I'm surveying our kingdom—a field of milkweed, lumber piles, bulldozed rubble—while waiting for Kal to pass me the first panel of roofing. Once we finish nailing them up here, we'll finally have a shelter that holds out the rain, and no way to get down except by sliding to the ladder, trying not to catch our overalls on a nail head. I don't know what the trees think about our dream to live a self-reliant life among them, but our parents think we're crazy. We could have had it easy in a brick house with appliances and a lawn, fulfilling the dream of their hardship generation. We received the benefits of all their dreams, thank you very much, but we are the do-your-own-thing generation.

We may be crazy, but at least we started with a firm idea of what our dream requires. A small clearing in a mixed woods, is what we told the realtors. A south slope, so the garden will thaw out early and drain well. A hill behind the site so we can build an earth-bermed passive solar house. As refugees from the oil shortage that surprised us into electing Jimmy Carter just last year, we're all about energy conservation. We want to try out these innovations on a dirt road in a rural town where old-timers and newcomers mingle. And one thing is for certain, we told the realtors: the price has to fit what we can pay cash for.

We thought of land as a blank space to start adult life all over again. But land is never blank, and its borders are imaginary lines that can't hold out a thing. Thanks to our new neighbors Eric and Laura, who directed us here when we knocked on their door, what we found in midcoast Maine was this overgrown field where old apple trees and junk buried all around a fallen cellarhole told us we weren't the first to bring our dream and our labor here. Hessians settled Guinea Ridge in 1777, but it was a nightmare that brought them to America when their fathers in Germany sold them to the British as mercenary soldiers. For their service, the sons received land here for a few guineas an acre and they stayed for a hundred years, until typhus wiped out the children in the 1870s. Now it's 1977, and our arrival displaced a family of porcupines who remain overseers of this place, inspectors of all things rubber and plywood. We join the crowd of people, animals, and plants who've taken root here, in what not all of us know as Knox County.

"Here it comes," Kal shouts as he passes the first long sheet of aluminum up the ladder on the north side. "Got it," I say, sliding it up along the rafters. How we managed to bring forth such a tall house is a mystery. When we used to visit the land, even in pouring rain, we felt sheltered by the pines I'm eye-to-eye with right now. The house we'd imagined would be cozy and low, built into the hillside, with pine siding vertical like the trees it was milled from. It took us two years to convince the absentee landowner to sell these acres, so we'd saved enough money from our jobs in New Hampshire—mine at an adult education program, Kal's at the county nursing home—to pay cash for the land and the building materials. We signed the deed, and the land was finally "ours." But now we know it was never really ours until we claimed it with our sweat, and shouts of rage against how a dream swirls from the heart, wild and free, but a plan is so stubbornly geometry, time, and money.

We're starting on the north side of the salt-box–style roof because it's low to the ground. We have no idea how we'll ever get the roofing nailed on the high, steep south side. Kal's grimy cap appears at the top of his ladder, and here comes my husband of two years, looking so much older than when we got here in May with our sketch of a house drawn to scale. We still don't know how much we don't know, but we do know we couldn't have gotten this far without David, our New Hampshire neighbor. Kal and David hadn't known each other as students at Harvard twelve years back, but we found ourselves living quite by accident next door to David and Anne in Canterbury. He dropped in one night last year and saw our drawing of the house in Maine.

"Windows aren't just pencil lines, ya know," David had snorted with disbelief that anyone could be so naïve about physical reality. "They need framing, and framing takes up space. See, like this." He whipped out a big flat pencil and scored thick lines down the blank expanse of south-facing windows. Suddenly each big window unit is three narrow ones. We're talking lumber, nails, caulking. Casement or double-hung, mullions or not. We didn't even know these words.

"Listen, want me to come up for two weeks in July?" he offered. He's as generous as he is gruff, this we already knew. He'd loaned us his roto-tiller to prepare a garden site between our house and his. When we showed up all distraught, holding out the tiller's broken blade for his inspection, he laughed and invited us in for dinner. Another time, on the Bicentennial in 1976, his truck rumbled into our driveway and he kidnapped us for a wild ride down Shaker Road, then brought us to his house and fed us lobsters and beer.

So we were grateful and a little nervous when he gave our drawing a slap with the pencil and said, "Have the foundation poured, and I'll help you get to the rafters." We did. He did. And now here we are, clambering up said rafters to tap the first nails into a roof that will transform these born-again trees into a place called home.

"Have the foundation poured" sounds easy enough, but turns out to be short-hand for a chain of events that begins with blank paper, a letter to a guy who does site work. Words set Borzoni's bulldozer in motion. He creates a gravel driveway, and plows a large area that will be the garden, all before we get here. Once we arrive, we learn that paper is not the way people operate around here. It's knock on doors, agree with a handshake, follow up with phone calls. Since we have no phone, many a night we sit parked in the VW seven miles from home, waiting for a return call at the phone booth in Union. Our plans have consequences we can't see, and it's a good thing we can't or we might have rolled that paper right back up and used it to swat flies.

Not that we ever doubt our downwardly-mobile move with mobile home in tow, a decrepit pink trailer someone sold us for cheap just to get rid of the eyesore. With friends Carol and Tommy (girls in the Volks, guys in the truck pulling Pinkie), we arrive in April. The first thing that happens is the trailer gets stuck making the sharp turn into the soft dirt of our new driveway. A plea for help brings the neighbor from up the road, who almost loses a finger checking the truck's fan belt. Shya is another one of those crazy hippies whose parents probably had something else in mind for him. He is ten steps ahead of us, because he's already built his house from timbers felled and hewn by hand. And more importantly he knows just the right balance of clutch and gas to yank Pinkie up the hill and across the grass to where she rests, no more changing views from her windows, no more need for wheels. The first night, we raise mugs of cheap wine to toast the wild grapevine just beyond the campfire. Next morning, back to New Hampshire for the rest of our stuff.

We arrive for good in a U-Haul packed like a milkweed pod ready to burst. At least with milkweed, you know what comes of the seed.

We, on the other hand, don't have a clue what we're in for, but we figure we're all set with our how-to books, half a cord of firewood and boxes of canning jars, an iron skillet and two water jugs. From Pinkie's windows we can see the furrows Borzoni's plow left, just beyond a young cherry tree with three trunks. We set the first pot of rice on the Coleman stove, and go over for a closer look at the soil where we'll fold the seeds of our sustenance. The garden will be, in every sense, our life.

What goes on inside the garden's borders is something we do know about, having raised our own food for three years now. Kal kneels down at the edge of the brown rectangle to stick a finger in the soil. It is solid sod. Fingers can write a letter to Borzoni asking him to plow, and plowing turns strips of raw earth grass-side down. But a finger can't penetrate sod, nor can a seed ever hope to grow in it. Not without Aldeverd, an old-timer from the next road over, coming to break it up with his harrow. Not without a rented tiller that shakes Kal to the teeth, and nearly topples him as he guides the roaring machine back and forth across the sloping site we searched so long to find. Not without the hands-and-knees labor of two people in mosquito nets digging out roots. And spreading the compost we hauled from our New Hampshire garden, and the manure a local farmer delivered during a freak May snowstorm.

Only then can we unroll the garden plan, drawn up last winter, and begin to plant. How many times will we come to find out that paper is an idiot who takes as gospel whatever the pencil says? Where the map commands "carrots," on the ground the hoe scrapes ledge. Where it spells out "cucumbers," we work all day to dig out a square boulder. "Beans" go along the bottom, just where we find a woodchuck hole, and they really love beans. And from all four edges of the vast, hand-worked garden, witchgrass begins its underground parade into the fertile soil.

Our dream is troubled by the wicked white roots, the overalls worn thin at the knees, gloves with no fingers left, bent tines on the spading fork, garden cart battered from hauling rocks. Our dream of a new start on adulthood awakens into the material world, where poplar offers itself in abundance. Poplar trees grow fast, smell sweet, rot soon. We rig a coldframe from poplar branches and plastic, to protect the seedlings and warm the yogurt. Erect a porch against the trailer, from poplar logs and screening, for respite from the blood-sucking insects. Construct an outhouse, from poplar and tin roofing. Hang a black plastic shower bag by a rope from a poplar tree. Poplar bean poles, poplar fence posts. Poplar stumps for campfire seats.

They call poplar "biscuit wood" around here. It burns hot and fast. In a woodstove. Which we lack. Coleman stove cookery leaves us hungry as monks. Beans, rice, tea, and nary a biscuit. We wait long for those first lettuce leaves, stretched to make a salad with dandelion, yarrow, violet. And longer, for peas and spinach. Finally, oh joy, the rush of zucchini is upon us. Our hunger is driven by a dream worth protecting from critters, insects, crows.

"Have the foundation poured," did he say? Not before weeks of clearing the house site with hand saws, and pulling a garden cart loaded with brush uphill into the woods. Finally Eric comes with his chainsaw and helps us finish off the job in a few hours. Then Borzoni returns with his machinery to impose straightness on the wild land. His backhoe uproots cedar trees, snacks on boulders, digs the hole in the ground where we will pour our money. I stand by and yell NO whenever the bulldozer gets too close to the bower of old lilacs. He teases me by pretending to go after them. "Aw, this place'll all come back clover next year," he assures us as we mourn the raw plain we've created. Even the money we hand over to him will grow back. After he goes, we celebrate with iceless gin-and-tonic in stoneware mugs, whooping and crying as dust swirls around the site in the hot July wind. We've been at it nine weeks.

From the scratching of pencils to the roar of diesel-powered equipment, we arrive at the day Dougie and his crew come to pour the concrete. The finished foundation rises two feet above grade. Sills and floor joists, subfloor and flooring will add more than another foot. This will not be a hobbit house after all, one small hop up from the ground. At least four steps will ascend to our door.

David's on his way, towing a camper-trailer with Anne and their two little girls, to help turn a stack of lumber into a house. He'll bring a chainsaw to cut the framing pieces, since there's no electricity here. We figure two weeks with David, and another two on our own, and we'll be out of the brutally hot pink trailer in time for canning season.

Pinkie was once a Queen. She was a top-of-the-line 1940s trailer, deep rose with a sharp white diagonal on each side. Round windows in the two doors. Arched ceiling, birch cabinets, windows with screens. One bedroom the size of a double mattress. Clothes storage in overhead cubbies. She was wired and plumbed, with light fixtures, kitchen sink and tiny bathroom. Good solid wheels.

Now she's thirty years old and she is derelict, her leaky roof patched with tar, a faded pink anachronism in this age of white vinyl trailer-homes. I am thirty, too, but I am not rotting from moisture in the walls. My door handles are not broken. Pinkie now lives engulfed in milkweed, whose dusty pink flowers match her fading metallic shell. She sags on the knoll overlooking a rough garden where we scratch out vegetables. We cook them on a Coleman stove balanced on crates. Pinkie has no water now, except in jugs we lug from a spring below the garden. Her rusty sconces hold no electric bulbs. A kerosene lamp glows through her windows in the evening. The screen door still keeps out mosquitoes, and lets in the sound of owls hooting, bullfrogs garumphing, poplar leaves tickling, all through the humid summer nights.

Pinkie was a Queen. Now she is a hot sardine can, housing our cramped life. Get up at 5 a.m., brew herb tea in a thermos, wrap a kettle of boiling beans and rice in a super-insulated box to cook all day, and go to work with heavy heart, tired legs, aching back. Pinkie is thirty and a deposed monarch. I am thirty, a servant to my dream.

David bursts onto the scene with his get-it-done energy. The first day, we bolt the bottom plate to the foundation, drilling holes by hand with a bit-brace and tightening the nuts with a ratchet wrench. Good tools help. We nail spruce sills to the plate, and the next day begin to span the cool cellar with sweet-smelling floor joists. It takes big swings of the hammer to drive the nails home. David goes bang bang bang bang, and the nail sings a little rising scale on its way in. We go bang ten times, and sometimes we go smash, and then we learn about another good tool, a cat's paw, for removing bent nails. When he stops to fuel the chainsaw for cutting more joists, David watches us hammer. "Cripes, guys, flex your wrist, won't ya? Use your shoulder!" He pulls the cord and the saw roars in the noonday heat. Doesn't he ever take a break?

Day three has us crawling all over the plywood subfloor, nailing our brains out. David can't get used to our book-learned ideas, like placing annular nails every two inches to keep squeaks out of the floor. "Two inches!" he complains. "Jeezum, a nail every foot will hold it down in a hurricane, ya know." So he puts in one every foot, and we tag along after him pounding the extras. Annular nails are good because they don't work their way out, but they're the devil to pull when bent. "Hit it from the top!" David barks. "No wonder they bend! Can't you see you're hammering at an angle?" He stops mid-afternoon for tea and banana bread that Anne brings down from their camper on the hill behind the house site. By the time Kal and I finish nailing and pulling out the bent ones, David's ready to get back to work. We stuff our mouth with banana bread, and go down on our knees until mosquitoes tell us to quit at dusk.

After great pain, a giddy joy erupts that night. The house is a big blond dance floor, booming a hollow rhythm under dusty boots. We unfold four beach chairs on the platform, and sit drinking Miller beer. We're miles off the ground, and this is only the first floor. How tall will this thing be? Then off to bed, each in our respective trailer, theirs with a propane refrigerator and stove, two sleeping girls stowed in the top bunk; ours crammed with tools, clothes, books, supplies. Morning comes too soon.

Next day is all about studs. Our choice of 2x6 lumber, instead of the standard 2x4s, mystifies David. We've read all about passive solar houses. This one will let the sun pour heat through south-facing windows to be absorbed by the concrete north wall. With the energy crisis in full swing, we want thicker walls to hold more of the heat inside.

"Who cares about oil prices?" David argues, gesturing toward the surrounding woods. "You're gonna heat with wood anyway."

"Wood we'll be cutting by hand with a two-person saw," explains Kal, to which David rolls his eyes.

"That's why God created the chainsaw," he retorts. "Anyway, you could practically heat this size house with a lightbulb!"

"No electricity," I point out.

"Okay, so heat it with that composting toilet you're so excited about. All that shit's gonna generate a lot of heat."

Dave's a whirring blade, and there's no shade here as we kneel on the floor to lay out studs for the first wall. Even Anne's mint tea doesn't cool us. We get her to check for plumb as we raise the wall. She calls, "Good!" as the bubble settles in the eye of the level, and we quickly hammer it to the edge of the platform. The emerging shape looks like the scale model, all right, but bigger than we ever dreamed.

And it all takes so much time. We learn the layered truth of a house, each round of the perimeter taking muscle and skill, plywood and nails, tar paper and staples. Slabs of money from our diminishing savings account. We'll wait to do insulation and siding after David leaves. Forget about finish flooring, or finish-anything, until the money starts to grow back.

David's on a two-week schedule. He's fast and furious with morning coffee streaming through his veins, faster and furiouser the higher we go. On rafter day, Kal and I get up extra early, and over granola with powdered milk and herb tea, we check the plan and compile a materials list. One of us drives to the pay phone in Union to call the lumberyard for a delivery. Come back and work all morning. Break for lunch. David sits under a pine tree with sandwiches Anne made, while we peel open the metal door to the 95-degree trailer and throw some food together. By the time we stagger out of Pinkie with our bowls of lettuce and leftover rice, he's antsy to start. "Let's go. Only a few more days. Kal, take my chainsaw and go cut rafters. Linda, you stack 'em by the ladder. I'll take 'em up."

Studs are one thing. You measure and cut. But rafters are complicated, with angles and notches we never understood in our carpentry textbook, and don't get even now that we've seen a sample. Kal holds his chopsticks in mid-air over the wooden bowl, and says, "You know I don't use a chainsaw, Dave."

David's about to blow his stack. He can't believe how much we don't know. "Oh, why don't you go do what you're good at?" he snaps. "Why try to be what you're not?" He hikes up his pants and straps on a nail belt. "Y'oughta stick to lifting nothing heavier than a pile of books!" He yanks on his cap and stalks away toward the site, then yells over his shoulder, "You guys should be working with people, not wood!" Anne shrugs sympathetically and clears away their plates.

David and Anne have always been so good to us, ever since we moved next door to them in Canterbury two years ago. They praised our garden and admired our bee hives, shared their raspberries, invited us to come sit on their deck and drink beer. We always respected David's know-how, the kind that comes from growing up on a farm. I guess he thinks men are born knowing tools, so Kal's don't-know-how confuses him. Kal is a man who grew up folding boxes in his parents' clothing store. In college, his job was making toast in the dining hall. And then he became a dean. In David's world, a man works beyond endurance with as much sweat as possible, and he's determined to make a man out of Kal.

David yanks the cord on the saw and starts cutting rafters. I'm the one who's supposed to drag them up the ladder. He watches me pressing shaky knees against the rungs as I climb, and changes his mind. "Get down off that ladder! Kal, you go up. Linda, you lug boards from the pile."

Kal's in no shape to go up the ladder, either, but down I come and up he goes. We are busted, and honestly don't know how we can keep working. What we do know is how far we still have to go. The house is an empty shell open to the sky. We have to accept the rules of this work site. David's the chainsaw guy. He assigns jobs, chooses the radio station, calls break-time and quitting-time. He is the boss. I'm the helper. Kal is the slave.

We couldn't frame this house without him, and sometimes, for a few minutes at a time, it's even fun. Today's his last day. We're gunning for the rafters. The aluminum roof will be up to us. Dave's strictly a shingle man himself. But we have a notion, as usual. Aluminum roofing comes in sheets and gets nailed to strapping, so there's no need for plywood under the roof, a considerable savings in time and material. Besides, we're seven miles from the volunteer fire department, so we want a fire-resistant roof like our hippie neighbors. Dave generously offers to come back for the windows, but not until we've put up the roof on our own. At the last second, he takes pity on us and helps nail the horizontal strapping to the rafters, but swears the aluminum roof is a big mistake. "The sound of the rain is going to drive you nuts."

Now they're all packed to go home, leaving the camper here for next time. He raises his eyes to the open roof as he jumps into the station wagon loaded with girls and gear. "Good luck!" he grins, and revs the engine. Gravel scatters on the dirt road, and he's gone. There is no silence more terrible than the one when your carpenter pulls out, leaving sheets of aluminum lying in a pile at the foot of a ladder.

The north side of the roof is low to the ground, first-floor–only window openings, concrete wall hugged by the earth berm. From the back, the house looks something like our dream, cozy and belonging to this place. The north aluminum went on fairly well yesterday. Now, on this hottest morning of the summer, we've come to the dreaded south roof, which has a long overhang Kal calls the "baseball cap." It's a wonder we never thought about how odd the overhang would look, but aesthetics wasn't a consideration. We were after another notion, designing with a protractor to keep the high June 21st sun out and allow the low December 21st rays all the way in to touch the concrete north wall. All very smart on paper. But now we're staring up at those high, bare rafters sticking way out over nothing, and wondering how to begin. Laura shows up from next door with a baby on her hip, a toddler by the hand, for her periodic inspection of our progress.

"It's gonna be a scorcher," she says, watching us strap on our tool belts. "You could wet your hats to keep cool up there." She eyes the rafters as we scuff sandpaper over our boot soles to give us a grip for climbing the slippery north slope to the ridge pole. We're in no mood to be very friendly this morning.

"I love those tall windows," she says, grabbing Heather to keep her from playing with the sharp scraps of aluminum scattered on the rocks, "but why no windows on the second floor?"

"It's going to be an attic," I say. "We're just going to live in the one room downstairs, and store whatever we don't need for each season in the attic."

"Oh. Are you going to have stairs?"

"No. Just a ladder. We don't want to waste any living space on stairs. The house is only 16 feet by 24."

"Won't you need an upstairs when you have children?"

"This building is going to be the garage and workshop once we build the real house," says Kal. He shoots me a look, like don't get into it. Secretly we're beginning to doubt our original plan, now that we've seen how much goes into even a small house. This surely will be The House after all. We aren't thinking about children. All we're thinking about is roofing. We start dragging some sheets of aluminum behind the house to where the ladder is. Laura just says, "Oh," and heads down the driveway with her brood.

David had excused me from high-altitude duty, but now there's no choice. I climb the ladder as if to the guillotine. We grapple our way up the north aluminum by fingertips leveraging off nail heads, and grab the ridge pole to pull ourselves to the peak. There's mostly nothing below the south rafters, just a few feet of house and then the two-story free fall from the overhang. My heart is pounding behind my teeth as we guide the first piece of aluminum down the south side.

We're already yelling at each other. I drop my hammer and it thunks on the rocks below. The thin metal we're crawling along is all there is between outside and inside, and it's burning hot as the sun rises over the sheltering pine trees. Kal starts tapping nails into the knotty strapping. Aluminum nails with rubber gaskets. They bend easily, and we learned yesterday that pulling them out leaves holes in the roofing that we'll have to caulk later, if we can find them. Or we'll find them over the years where the rain leaks in.

We get the first piece nailed as far as we can reach, and now we're screaming at each other about how to attach the overhang without slipping down head-first onto the rocks. The answer pulls up into the driveway. It's big burly Borzoni, looking tiny down there next to a toy truck. He cranes up at us, and offers to hold Kal by the ankles. What choice do we have? He scoots up the ladder, boots going cring-crang as he bounces up the north roof and finds us clinging in sweaty fear to the ridge. Kal flops face-down, his belly sizzling on the hot metal as Borzoni grabs his feet. I watch my husband overhanging the edge between life and death with a hammer in his hand.

We manage to get all but the last panel on that way before Borzoni has to leave. We go down for water, and that's when we look up and notice each roof panel has gone on slightly out of square, thanks to misplacement of the very first piece. By the rules of geometry, the out-of-square got bigger and bigger as we moved along the rafters. The last panel juts out at the bottom edge, and doesn't quite meet the ridge at the top. We go back up the ladder to check it out, and it really seems like Kal's going to rip out his hair. He's cursing and shaking his fist at the sky. The surrounding pines have never seen anything like it. As for me, I'm scared shitless by his rage. It starts to rain, and we tear into each other, two voices shouting from the rooftop until swarming mosquitoes drive us down the ladder. We flee to the trailer and huddle in our sleeping bag listening to rain on Pinkie's roof. At least there's one roof here that keeps us dry.

Next day, still yelling at each other over every move, we look down from the roof and see Eric sauntering up the driveway wearing a nail belt and straw hat. "Need some help?" he asks, later admitting he heard our shouts a quarter-mile away at his house. When he sees the patch we've cut with tin-snips to cover the gap, he sees why. He has an aluminum roof, too, and knows how to lope up the slippery slope chimpanzee-style. He straddles the house as if it were a giant horse, hammering the ridge cap on as he hikes himself along by the seat of his pants. He doesn't know he's saved our marriage.

We thought we'd be all finished with the house by canning time in late August. Instead, I set up the Coleman stove on a table under an oak, and process tomatoes and corn *al fresco*, carrying the jars down a ladder to store in the new cellar. In September the onions, garlic, potatoes, and squash move in before we do. An October cold snap brings us inside with only a blanket for a door. The windows, thanks to Dave's merciful second visit, are in.

Our vegetables, maturing in a known number of days, teach us the difference between natural time and carpenter's time. The time formula for a building project goes like this: take x as the time you plan on (four weeks, in our case), then double it (2x=eight weeks), then upgrade the x to y (eight months). We spend the winter inside, nailing up the pine wall boards from a pile stowed under the bed. We have a door with a hand-made oak latch, a metal chimney for the wood cook-stove. The cellar keeps our milk cold, and a kerosene lamp casts a warm glow at night.

Sometimes you wake up from a dream exhausted, as if you've accomplished some feat. You are changed. Nothing looks the way you remember it when you went to sleep. One winter day, we hike up the hill behind Eric and Laura's with new friends, and Grobe says, "Look, there's Kal and Linda's!" We follow his pointing finger through the bare oaks, and far below, across a marsh, see a tiny blond house with blue window frames.

Juniper-blue stain, and the consequent turpentine, were just the first thing we swore we'd never do, then did. David scoffed at our idea of leaving the house all natural. "Better stain that trim, or watch it rot!" A house is not an idea but a life that grows from the inside, like us. At one year, true to Laura's prediction, a staircase to a finished bedroom for us to share with the baby. At four years, an addition as big as the original house, with a living room and attached woodshed downstairs, Noah's bedroom and a study upstairs, the light shining through its eyes no longer kerosene but solar-powered. At eleven years old, the house sprouts a small dining room and custom-built kitchen cabinets. The boards on the outside age from blond to dark grey with streaks of butterscotch and silver, blending the house into the hillside where ever taller pines are joined by flourishing oaks and pretty poplars.

The inside of the inside of the house we built is our marriage, hard won, comforting. From the first, it was a marriage rooted in a dream. The seed sprouted and grew into a trunk, a journey to find the place to branch out. From branch and leaf, back down to nourish the root, we become a family sheltered on the edge between know and don't-know. And it's a good thing that don't-know is most of it, or there'd be nothing left to dream.

The Apple Doesn't Fall Far from the Tree

This could be my story, and it could be Noah's. Mother and son, we're two shoots growing from the same root. This much I know: the story stems from a certain gnarly apple tree down by the spring we hauled water from while we were building our homestead and raising Noah. When he left for college, the spring went dry after two years of drought, and we had to drill a well. One-hundred-twenty feet down, the new well taps deeper into the same vein that feeds the old spring, which shows how a journey draws strength from the same unseen root no matter how far it travels. The water travels farther now, too, pumped to the house with solar power. We don't carry it anymore from under the old apple tree.

This starts as my story because the apple tree helped me give birth. I walked under the tree's low branches every day to fill the water jugs. That October, the tree was heavy with red fruits, despite dead branches and insect-riddled trunk. I can't say I really noticed the apples as I did my daily chore, jugs hanging from a yoke and a swelling belly in the middle. The last day of pregnancy, three weeks past the due date, my tired bones just could not support another forty pounds of water. I lay on the couch and watched an early snow fall, while my friend Wendy went down for the water and came back to fix tea. It took nine months plus the extra three weeks to submerge me in the life I was carrying. I was, finally, a vessel full to the brim.

The next day this story became Noah's, and not mine only. Labor began at midnight, the tenth of October, 1979. I figured by 8 a.m. I'd be sitting up in bed eating breakfast while Kal held the newborn babe in a bundle. We left for the hospital right away, a forty-minute drive to Belfast in light snow. Eight hours later, I was barely dilated, and my waters hadn't broken. At each hard contraction, Kal coached me to blow out, out, out, and I focused on the fleur-de-lis design of my hospital gown. Our birthing teacher had warned us that women go crazy during transition, the last stage of labor. Sometimes they have visions or babble incoherently, try to jump out a window or yell obscenities at their husband, say they don't want to have a child at the very moment it's way too late. But we were in shape. We were trained to blow into a bag, suck ice chips, do back massages, all that. And how could it be harder than what we'd already done, building a house, raising a garden, hauling water?

This isn't the story of my labor, though. If I wanted to write that, I would not have waited until well into a mother's menopause and a son's manhood. It took me this long to find the story I want to tell, how the apple tree guided us into everything that came next.

I did want to jump out the window during transition. I did curse my husband. I forgot I was pregnant, and didn't know what that searing pain in the small of my back was. I should have squatted, but instead I thrashed on a bed in need of a straightjacket, and eyed the window with its promise of escape. At the height of a contraction, when I just couldn't stand it anymore, I was suddenly lifted into a clear vision of the apple tree by the old spring, covered with red apples. The contraction subsided, and so did the vision. Then the next contraction came. A circle of light dilated in my skull to reveal the apple tree again. I hadn't noticed the tree all that much, but it had noticed me. Now it kindly offered a safe place to jump out of the present and into eternity. At each contraction, it held me in its old, bent branches, until finally the nurse wheeled me to the delivery room.

"Where are we going?" I snarled, and when she showed me the mirror by my feet, the dark crown pressing at the opening, I tried to sit up. "What is *that*?"

"The head."

"The head?"

"You're having a baby!"

"A baby?"

"Don't push," the nurse directed. We were waiting for the doctor to get there. I pushed. Out came a head with the cord around its neck. "Don't push, don't push, don't push!" She deftly uncoiled the loop from around the neck just in time. I pushed, and a baby slid out into her hands. "It's a boy!" she exclaimed, and Kal danced a shuffle around the delivery room in his paper slippers. "It's Noah!" we both cried.

"The apple doesn't fall far from the tree," Kal's Russian grandfather always said. The old tree gave birth to a family of three with one story shooting up from the root. "It is a tree of life to them that lay hold of it." Mother and son sure did lay hold of the saving tree that day, and we were delivered into life.

The next thing I knew, I was delivering Noah to Hebrew school at the synagogue in Rockland. Driving a second-grader to Hebrew school is not something I ever thought I'd do. My cousin David says I was the least likely person in our extended family to raise a Jewish child. David and the other cousins on my father's side thrived as a little enclave of Old World tradition, centered around my father's mother, the grandmother I hardly knew. She was stocky and drab, with her hair in a bun, dark dress and cloddy shoes. They ate kippers and corned beef, and had cupboards full of dishes for meat, dishes for dairy foods, dishes used only at Passover. Their Passover seder went on for hours, all in Hebrew, and the kids were banished to the other room if we giggled or squirmed. Their bookcases sagged with musty volumes in Hebrew and Yiddish. They walked to *shul* on Saturdays.

I walked to high school football games on Saturdays, and went to dances at the YMCA on Friday nights, while Sabbath candles burned in my cousins' homes. They burned in my home, too, but my cousins were Jewish and we were American. They observed the Sabbath as a special day of rest, study, and prayer. We lit candles, then went about our business. Our synagogue was not called a *shul*, not even a synagogue. We called it "temple," and we attended "Saturday School," not Hebrew school. My boy friends had Bar Mitzvahs, but the girls had confirmation instead, just like our Christian friends. After confirmation, I wriggled out of Saturday School because I didn't like the two rabbis and couldn't get the hang of Hebrew, despite my gift for other languages. An all-'round suburban American girl, I was finished being Jewish by the time I left home in Rochester for Cornell. There, I fell in love with choral music and church bells and bacon. I studied medieval Latin. I never dated Jewish guys, until Kal. But this is not the story of my flirtation with Christianity, any more than it's the story of my labor. This is the story of how Noah entered the world through an old apple tree, and joined his parents on their Jewish journey from assimilation and alienation, back to the root.

The 1960s and '70s brought lots of disaffected young Jews to Maine, stirring a streak of borscht into the beanpot of small-town Maine. We were going back-to-the-land, not back-to-Judaism, though driven by the same pioneering spirit that transformed Israel from a desert into a garden. But we didn't see ourselves as part of that tradition. We invented the idea of living on the land, building shelter, gardening, and forming community with like-minded folk, didn't we?

While so many of our generation quit the city, the university, the family, the synagogue, and landed in rural places, there was another sphere of radical change we didn't know about yet. In New York, Philadelphia, California, and elsewhere, certain young rabbis were bringing to light an earlier version of the Jewish people. Our people were shepherds, farmers, foragers, healers, long before we were scholars. We became "the people of the book" only when we needed something portable to hold us together. By the time our generation was born in America, the book no longer did it for some of us. The calendar of nature-based holidays reminds us that we are also a people of the land, celebrating every new moon, every season of planting and harvest, the turning of the year from dark to light, the pledge to care for the earth. Kal and I embraced a do-it-yourself Judaism focused on the very local natural world. The attraction to growing our own food was an ethnic memory, for hadn't our ancestors lived as peasants, growing cabbages, beets, and onions?

The parents of all us Jewish hippies in remote outposts fretted, because how would their grandchildren be Jewish? Judaism is understood by most as a communal religion centered in the Old World village or the New World urban neighborhood, where a *minyan*, a quorum of ten adults, could easily be mustered to hold services. Kal and I had yet to produce the grandchild our parents worried about, and we weren't looking for a Jewish community. But, it turns out, the Jewish community found us.

We were sitting on the lawn of the Camden library overlooking the pretty harbor our first September in Maine, two years before Noah's arrival. We needed a break from our house-building frenzy twenty miles inland. I was napping under the big maples while Kal leafed through the local paper.

"Hey," Kal lifted the newspaper off the grass, closer to his face. "'High Holiday services will be held at the synagogue on Willow Street in Rockland,'" he read aloud.

"Synagogue? Rockland?" I raised myself up on an elbow. "Are you joking? Rockland is such a Norman Rockwell kind of place. How would Jews ever have gotten there?"

Turns out they got to Maine long before the great wave of immigration that brought our ancestors through Ellis Island to the Lower East Side of New York City in the 1890s. These earlier Jews sailed from Europe before the Revolutionary War as ship's provisioners, and travelled around coastal Maine peddling all manner of goods, from tinware to clothing. Before 1790, the "Hebrews" settled in Rockland, establishing businesses and professions. By 1912, when they purchased a church building for $100, they numbered 250. Their descendants still belong to the congregation in Rockland. We learned all this later. First we had to find the white clapboard synagogue where Rosh Hoshanah, the Jewish New Year, would be observed with a visiting rabbi, the paper said.

We showed up as strangers, but before we even took our place in a pew, we were showered with offers of lunch, used furniture, and all kinds of advice. Maybe it was Kal's beard, or simply our youth that endeared us so readily to them. The twenty-family congregation was too small to hire a rabbi, so we soon found ourselves organizing holiday events and leading services, and eventually Kal became the Hebrew teacher for a dozen children. Kal had acquired his knowledge of Hebrew growing up in a small-town Jewish community himself, in Claremont, New Hampshire. He was the only son, expected to attend services led by a series of rabbis who came and went. He continued Hebrew school past his Bar Mitzvah because he had a crush on the rabbi's daughter. His religious life ended with the first Hillel service he attended at Harvard. At age 20, on leave from Harvard, he went to live on a kibbutz in Israel when he was bumming around Europe and needed a place to stay warm once winter came. They put him to work planting in an orchard, where he wandered lost for hours with a banana tree balanced on his shoulder. He became fluent in Hebrew. Israel was not about religion, for him. It was about learning to plant trees, a skill that would serve him well on our future homestead. Who knew that Hebrew would come in handy, too?

Two years later, we showed up at Rosh Hoshanah services accompanied by our Quaker-Jewish obstetrician, because I was greater than great with child. A month later, we invited the community to our place to celebrate our first-born son. The next year, they all came out again, this time for the harvest festival of Sukkot. We constructed a *sukkah* (booth) out of poplar poles, like everything else around the place, and decorated it with corn stalks and pumpkins from the garden. Traditionally, Jews wave a *lulav* made of palm, myrtle, and willow branches bound together. We all crowded into the shelter to say the blessings and wave our Maine *lulav* made of pine, lilac, and cedar. Instead of sniffing an *etrog*, a lemon-like fruit that grows in the Middle East, we passed an apple hand-to-hand. We were a community ripe for some home-grown Judaism.

There were a few Jewish kids in the Rockland schools, but Noah was the only Jew in our local Appleton Village School. Starting with kindergarten, and for eight Decembers until they all went off to the regional high school in Camden, Kal and I were invited to come share Chanukah with Noah's class. The scene never changed, though after a few visits the kids got over their shock at the news that Jesus was a Jew. We pulled open the glass door and stepped into a hallway bedecked with Christmas lights, wreaths, and ribbons, the sound of carols streaming from the gym. And who should we bump into but Santa himself, right there in the main office. A menorah couldn't hold a candle to all this Christmas hubbub, but Noah's classmates were impressed that he was allowed to strike the match. They liked the gold chocolate coins. *Latkes* were not a hit; who would choose potato pancakes with home-made applesauce over the rich treats of Christmas?

"Christmas is a religious holiday," we quietly reminded the principal and the music teacher year after year. Even introducing Chanukah wasn't really appropriate. "This is a public school."

"Of course you're right," they agreed, and missed the point by adding one Chanukah song to the concert, and a cut-out menorah to the front bulletin board. Noah had already hit the truth as a preschooler when he saw the world divided into our family and "the Christmas people." The school hit the truth about Noah when they gave him the leading role in the Christmas pageant one year. He played an alien who landed from outer space and didn't know what all the fuss was about. "Ho-ho-ho, mer-ry-chris-mas?" he learned to intone like a programmed computer.

I remembered being an alien child. Christmas filled me with a longing not assuaged by my mother's annual offering of a candy cane, or even her eventual willingness for us to hang a stocking. I helped decorate my best friend's tree, and when I came home and asked Mom why we didn't believe in Jesus, she said, "Because we're Jewish." The unanswered question persisted all through my childhood.

"We were waiting for the Messiah," I put it to the rabbi, "so why didn't we accept Jesus?"

The rabbi, well-known for his work with young people, answered, "Because we didn't."

My attraction to Christmas slowly became an attraction to Jesus. I brought a Hebrew Bible to my friend's Sunday School, and the teacher was so impressed with it she asked to display it in the library, giving me a little picture of Jesus in exchange. I kept the kind face hidden in my dresser drawer, under a pile of sweaters. In high school, I purchased a bible that contained not just the five books of Moses, but the New Testament, too, with Jesus' words printed in red.

"Jesus said some very wise things," I ventured to the rabbi, still hoping to get my question answered, why we didn't believe in Jesus.

"Our tradition is ancient," he responded, which did nothing to stop me from heading off in my own direction—away.

In college, I got my fill of Christmas by going home with a boyfriend whose family was all cookies and eggnog and candlelit church services. "She doesn't *look* Jewish," his parents whispered, which I took as praise. I got my fill of Jesus, too, by electing to study medieval art and theology. The boyfriend and I got married when I graduated. A week before the wedding, I overheard my grandmother comforting my distraught mother with, "I think she's marrying Christmas, Harriet."

Christmas and I eventually got divorced, and by the time I met Kal, I'd come to admire Jesus as a disruptive revolutionary. I understood why the Jews of his time didn't embrace him as their Messiah, any more than the hawkish politicians of ours listened to the unsettling message of peace activists. Kal and I chose to live in a place where we could worship evergreen trees every day, not just at Christmas. Way back in, without electricity, our Decembers were all about family time, not racing around shopping or stringing the house with flashing lights.

When Noah was two, before his sojourn at the Appleton Village School, we got solar electricity, and a black-and-white TV. One night I was frying *latkes* when I heard the Muppets singing carols and realized that my child, sitting in the dark watching *Sesame Street*, was getting his first dose of Christmas. I went in to join him. He observed the spectacle with curiosity, and grasped right away that even Big Bird belonged to that other clan. The day after Christmas we all went out to lunch. The waitress asked him, "Was Santa good to you?" Our two-year-old explained in a level voice, "We are Jewish. We don't have Christmas." She recoiled in horror. In a world of "Christmas people," the joke in our family became that Santa Claus always comes down the vent pipe to use our composting toilet in a house where no one will hassle him.

By the time Noah reached second grade, just learning to write on wide-ruled paper, he was proud to be a Jew. It gave him a kind of edge. He was special, the only Jew. He was special to me, too, the only child. We began a Thursday routine that lasted for six years. I picked him up at school with a peanut butter sandwich and apple juice, and we drove the half-hour to Rockland for Hebrew school. While other kids were playing ball or watching TV, Noah was sitting in the synagogue basement wearing a *yarmulke*, learning to read and write backwards.

Hebrew isn't just backwards because it's written from right to left. That much he mastered early, astonishing his regular teacher with a story about Hebrew school written entirely backwards, from right to left with all the English letters in mirror image. Our trips to Hebrew school took us backwards in a more important sense. Driving the rusted red Volkswagen twenty miles east to Rockland, I was driving him back in time to encounter the world of Eastern Europe. Then we'd drive west, through Appleton, to our present life in Burkettville, far from other Jews, which our ancestors in their villages with a house of prayer in the center could not have imagined. I was willingly driving him back to what I had resisted, and he was eager to go.

Kal had taught Hebrew school for five years, but by now Liz was the teacher. She was warm and welcoming, so different from my Hebrew teachers who kept a tight rein on us in classrooms that looked just like regular school, except the maps on the wall depicted the ancient Middle East, the alphabet chart on the wall was the aleph-bet. I got into trouble for giggling, passing notes, and never knowing the answer, unlike regular school where I was a model student. The only relief, after two hours, was joining the whole congregation for the Sabbath service in progress. My favorite part was the walk from the school wing to the sanctuary through an arched hallway that reminded me of a Christian monastery.

Liz smiled a lot, and hugged the kids when they arrived. They sat at the long table eating crackers and learning the aleph-bet, songs, prayers, and rituals. Liz used the table for rolling out dough, too, to bake Chanukah cookies or a Purim pastry called Hamentaschen, little triangles filled with jam. They made costumes and posters for each holiday, and learned to observe the moon and the seasons. Most of the time, I just dropped Noah off with a "Have fun!" Living twenty miles from town meant packing every trip with errands. I came back to pick him up, and stood outside the door to listen or chat with other parents, but often I found myself drawn to the stairway. I tiptoed up to the empty sanctuary, dark except for the eternal light over the Ark that holds the Torah. Quiet except for the muffled sound of kids downstairs. There was something thickly palpable in the sanctuary when all the prayerbooks were closed, all the prayer shawls folded on a rack. I sat in the back pew and closed my eyes. I felt none of the intimidation that passed for awe when I was a child. None of the why-aren't-we-Christian resentment, the please-answer-my-questions frustration. I looked at the light over the Ark and closed my eyes again. I was gone, until the knocking radiator brought me back, and I went downstairs to meet Noah.

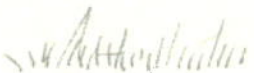

When Noah was one day old, we drove him to our tiny home in the woods. We called him "the almond-eyed boy," because no matter how long Kal walked him back and forth, his eyes stayed open, as if he perceived a presence in shapes we hardly noticed. We'd been trained to birth a baby, but not to care for one. My mother couldn't come help because she had no idea how to function in a house with water jugs and a wood cookstove. Lynne, up the road, had four boys, and she worked her magic on Noah by slinging him over her knee when he was crying. He needed us to learn tricks like that, so he began training us by crying until we got it right. Crying and crying, that first day home, as we rocked the cradle, added blankets, changed his diaper, picked him up, walked with him, fed him, sang to him. Finally we wore out. We propped him on pillows in the center of our double bed and snuck out. He stopped crying instantly. We peeked in to check. Is he still alive? He lay on the pillow with open eyes, moving his fingers in the air. He was content to be left alone in this fascinating new place where the dark ceiling met the square skylight, the dim curtained windows let in cracks of light.

He was seeing something we couldn't see because we labelled it "the window" or "the sun." A few months later, I saw it, too. I was walking with Noah on my back along the frozen dirt road one December afternoon. It started to snow. I ducked under an old hemlock and sat cross-legged on dry leaves at the base of its five trunks. I put Noah on my lap, a warm bundle in his pale blue snowsuit with a pointed hood, and we looked out at the snow falling beyond dark sheltering boughs. He sat stock still and watched with his almond eyes the snowflakes fall on the road, white on dark, and the feathery hemlock boughs that fringed our view, dark against light. But he saw something behind the flakes and the boughs, and I saw it, too. A nameless presence that was more like a sound, a whisper of snowflake and wind. Sitting with my chin on his head, I felt him go out of himself through his hooded crown, back to where he'd so recently come from.

We sat under the hemlock and saw God. The one who gets obscured by the namings of everyday life. The one who fills the sanctuary when all the books are closed. The same one who brushed my cheek when I was young, and smiled at the questions no one would answer, and waited for me to pipe down and listen. A journey came clear under the hemlock with a bundled son in my lap. My journey, and Kal's. Together we would plant this little wrapped root-ball, not knowing what to expect from a tree that brings forth the fruit of who you are.

An apple doesn't fall far from the tree. The most it can do is roll down hill. So our do-it-yourself Jewish observance was recognizably the same as what we each grew up with, though as different as homemade pie is from a bakery one. In the temple I grew up in, only the rabbi, the cantor, and the family of the Bar Mitzvah boy regularly stood on the *bima* up front. It was a fearsome place, with modern brass-sculpted doors that depicted Moses reaching for the Ten Commandments, and an eternal light in the form of a burning bush. The opportunity to disgrace one's family was readily available, not to mention the wrath of God.

Being on the *bima* at the Rockland synagogue wasn't scary to us three. Except for occasional visiting rabbis, our community's services were run by members, and we didn't always know what we were doing. Once, Kal was leading a Simchat Torah service assisted by me and baby Noah. Simchat Torah marks the completion of the annual reading of the Torah, ending with *Deuteronomy*, the last of the five books of Moses, then looping back to the beginning of *Genesis*. While we were busy re-rolling the sheepskin scroll, Noah crawled under the curtain and discovered the cord that electrifies the eternal light. Eternal. Never goes out. Just as Kal began to read, "In the beginning, God said, Let there be light...," Noah pulled the plug and the sanctuary went dark.

We were the blind leading the blind. Sometimes the blind can see better than the learned. We wrestled in the dark with a shape we call God. As a child I felt a nameless presence in trees that whispered and twinkled. As I grew older, I wanted to know more. Religion seemed like rules, not answers, and even if someone kind had taken me in hand, even if my father had passed on his Orthodox learning as I now wish he had, I probably would have resisted. I had to find my own way to the Tree of Life, with the help of Kal and Noah.

The way is "within you, within you, within you," Swami Muktananda chanted and waved a peacock feather at the meditation retreat Kal and I had attended when I was seven months pregnant. Like so many of our generation of spiritual pilgrims, we began with Transcendental Meditation and moved on to other practices, like Siddha Yoga. What were we all looking for? We'd been given every material comfort our parents longed for in hard times, but we wanted the deep invisible. "God is within you as you," Muktananda taught.

Seek no further than to "see God in each other." That sounded too easy. Even after the arduous journey to "find a home in ME." (as a friend cleverly put it when we moved to Maine), we didn't grasp Muktananda's teaching that to look outside yourself for fulfillment causes suffering. His lesson was reinforced when we took the newborn Noah to Boston to be blessed by the guru. Just as we arrived, Muktananda decided to go into silence until his return to India. "But we drove all the way from Maine to get a blessing for our baby!" No. He would not see us. We got in the car, a couple of vegetarian hippies with babe in arms, and drove to Cambridge for a hamburger at Bartley's. In the end, does it matter if Noah was blessed with a peacock feather or a Bartley's burger? He came into our family from an apple tree, and landed where we were busy making a home. An apple is just passing through. The way home is within you, within you, within you.

I say this is our story. Yet how would Noah tell it? He was a willing companion on our family journey. Ours was a chosen Judaism he took for normal, but there are customs, like the Bar Mitzvah, he had no choice about. The service opens with the parents and grandparents draping the son in a *tallit*, or prayer shawl, symbolically placing Jewish tradition on the shoulders of the next generation. Noah was still so small that the fringes touched the floor. He stepped up on a stool to chant his Torah portion from "Noach," the chapter in *Genesis* that tells the story of his namesake. "And Noah was a righteous man. He walked with God."

He may have walked with God, but he drove with Mom. To Hebrew school and home again hippety-hop, learning the language of our ancestors. As for me, I know five languages, but couldn't remember the Hebrew alphabet for the life of me. I did not join Noah with his flash-cards and workbooks. I learned no more in those six years of driving than I already knew—the blessings, songs, and rituals for Sabbath and holidays, and the traditional foods. Hebrew, to me, was the language of our fathers. Our mothers spoke kugel, challah, and borscht. My sense of being half a Jew, the mother half, intensified when our travels ended and Kal began training Noah for his Bar Mitzvah.

I could hear them upstairs practicing in Noah's room. Even a good father does to a son what his own father did to him. Kal's father (also good) always pushed Kal to perform well in public, or bring shame on his parents. Kal's father's father, Morris, was the one who said "the apple doesn't fall far from the tree." No doubt *his* father in Russia said it, too, which may explain why Morris ran away and boarded a ship for America at age 13. That apple better be brilliant, boy, dropping under the tree for all the world to judge our family by.

As the Bar Mitzvah day approached, I sensed this masculine heritage bearing down on them. We took on too much. A do-it-yourself Bar Mitzvah placed Kal in the position not only of father, hair-raising enough, but tutor and rabbi, for he would lead the service himself. I heard the mounting anxiety in Kal's voice as he put the pressure to Noah the same as he'd received from his father. *Chant as if you know it even if you don't (but you better know it soon).* I felt Noah's resistance, guilt, and fear making him smaller and smaller. Who could ever work hard enough with that pressure-cooker hissing away? I muffled the sound of their drama with a pillow over my head. Thank God I was born a girl!

We are all girls in my family. My two sisters and I felt sorry for Dad. We did our best to be sons. Yet how could I be a son if my father didn't teach me Hebrew? Now I see it's not about Hebrew. It's not about what a parent did or didn't do. It's about this Tree of Life—these Jewish teachings—that even a girl can lay hold of, in her own way, for her own reasons. After Noah's wonderful Bar Mitzvah, after he grew up and left home, and the well went dry, and we drilled a new one to tap a deeper vein, I had my own reason for learning Hebrew. I dropped my one apple, and now I'm headed down to the root within me.

My aging parents moved out of their house in Rochester, and were languishing in a brand-new retirement community. We sisters watched helplessly as our mother slid down into depression, and then lymphoma and chemotherapy. Our father, six years older, saw the writing on the wall, and started down the chute himself. He toppled over a few times, and because Mom was too sick to help him, he ended up in the Jewish Home for the Aged. Within a month, Mom moved in with him. She got better. He died.

I'd seen it coming, and wanted to be ready to say Kaddish for them when they died. Kaddish is a mourner's prayer that never mentions death. It declares that life is holy. I was still only half a Jew, the half that cooks and lights candles and abets the son's initiation. The duty to say Kaddish for my parents was a chance to become whole. I began to study Hebrew from a workbook I found on Noah's shelf after he left for college. I finally learned the aleph-bet and practiced the letters by sounding out prayers. I memorized the Kaddish, then moved on to other prayers. I even began to understand the words. I was ready by the time Dad died.

Learning Hebrew isn't just an act of filial piety. It's about survival in crossing the generational divide. I'm a middle-aged woman watching my child become an adult, my parents become children. Am I up to the task of being an elder on the tree? Saying the ancient words expresses a will to survive. The Holocaust was kept secret from us kids in the 1950s, but as I learn more, I see that when entire families perish, no one is left to say Kaddish. It's up to us to plant our children in Judaism. We're more than just the apples. We are the tree.

I learned Hebrew the do-it-yourself way, without driving to Rockland. But it is the same eastward route I travelled with Noah, back to the ancient root. Meanwhile, just like Kal at 20, Noah at 20 went east to Israel. On January 2, 2000 we watched our boy's plane rise into the air and head for the ancestral land. A month later, a young man wearing a *yarmulke* came through the airport gate. We three burst out laughing. The tree bore fruit!

The rest of this story will be his to tell, with chapters that trace his own Jewish way, and verses that sing of a son becoming his mother's teacher. We're still driving along together toward the eternal light. After the trip to Israel, he returned to Amherst College to complete a major in religion (primarily Buddhism), and pursue an actively Jewish life. I stayed home practicing prayers, and when he visited, he brought us his passion for keeping the Sabbath holy, for saying a blessing before and after eating the bounty of our garden, for seeking justice by every possible path.

This part is not my story, but if I were writing it, I'd mark the year 2001 as the moment that galvanized his solidarity with humankind. He graduated from college, and in late August took a job in lower Manhattan working as a legal advocate for poor people. On September 11th, he came up out of the stalled subway in Brooklyn, not quite believing what he heard on the street. He ducked into a *halal* market to get some water. Standing at the counter with a crowd of Muslim customers, he watched on TV as the towers collapsed. Right away he feared the global consequences. Under a storm of falling pens and scorched paper blown east from the World Trade Center, he made it back to his apartment. His life journey, it seems to me, begins with this walk.

Or did it begin way back as a baby in Maine, huddled in a blue snowsuit under the hemlock with me, watching the whirlwind? All I know is that on September 11th, a mother's Hebrew lessons melted into prayer itself. Same words, but the difference is intention. The difference is hope. Noah was spared. He walks with God.

Dual Household

Nothing speaks more eloquently of human endeavor than a garden set in the middle of a wild place. A house, with its concrete base, lines straight and plumb, slanted roof ready to throw off the weather, is a stay against the wild. But the four edges of a garden, even if fenced, can't keep out the riot of weeds waiting beyond the perimeter. What it takes is dedication to a foolhardy notion that *this garden is ours*.

So it's with dirt-caked knees that I affirm my intention this early May morning, crawling along the bottom edge of the garden. I rip lush weeds from the steaming brown soil where soon we'll plant corn and beans. How utterly unnatural a large expanse of earth with no plants growing in it! This irony epitomizes the choice we made in following our dream to this place. To live in the wild, the first thing we did was cut down trees and hire John Borzoni to dig a cellar with his noisy backhoe. To make a home in nature, we had to evict the partridges and whippoorwills who got here first. We opened the soil and picked out every visible root so our pampered vegetables would thrive.

It's ruthless, this edge thing, but it pays off. For thirty years now, we've held back the insurgent plant-life that threatens our food. Vigilance is a comic routine to which keeping the garden edge weeded is only the prologue. Later acts—like stopping raccoons from eating the corn before we do—involve hanging dirty laundry from the stalks, pouring a trail of urine all around the patch, touching the corn silks daily to leave a human scent, and if all else fails, erecting a solar-powered motion detector. Keeping the edge sharp was a choice we didn't even know we'd made. Inspired by articles in *Organic Gardening,* we found the cute little map of Gene Logsdon's Ohio homestead appealing. A green background represented the lawn around his house and goat barn and chicken coop, vegetable garden and orchard, perennial beds and shade trees. We fell for the layout, not knowing our choice would keep us mowing and clipping for the rest of our life.

Choice has consequences, and I am living proof as I crawl along the garden edge, early morning sun on my back, tossing clumps of grass into a white bucket. I brush the first black flies away from my eyelids and look up the slope to admire thriving pea vines and garlic shoots, and imagine the other vegetables soon to sprout from this place where no weed stands a chance. The hill rises gently toward the cherry tree that was here when we came, its triple trunk reduced in these decades to one curvaceous survivor towering over the garden. Past the cherry tree, there's a stone wall weighted with the old grapevine we found here, its fruits now neatly preserved as jelly and juice in the cellar. Beyond the grapes, I see the roof of a small barn where the pink trailer once sat rusting and sinking into its wheels. Tool shed, raspberry patch, orchard. All this would go under if not for me and this white bucket filling up with errant clover, if not for Kal and the lawnmower. The doorstep of the house would soon be engulfed in mint. Asparagus bed, pear and apple trees, the old well with a faded green pump, all would disappear under milkweed in our absence.

Down here at the bottom of all this endeavor, I'm tracing the edge of human history. History has an edge because we humans don't quite blend in. We live by ideas. We fight for control, even if we have to go down on our knees to get it. Dragging my bucket, I'm a parable of ambition, acting out the story we each tell by the choices we make. HERE I willingly commit body and time to grow my dream. Let the rest be wild, and obey its own rules. All but the one rule. Whoever crosses this line goes in the bucket. This square is mine.

Even from way down below the garden, I hear the phone ring at the house. I run for it, and it's one of my students. A few of them want to come help spread compost in the garden today, and they need directions for the hour-long drive from the college.

Thirty years ago, after Belknap College went bankrupt, I never thought I'd be a professor again, let alone host students at our backwoods homestead. We planned to raise chamomile blossoms for Celestial Seasonings tea company. Really. Until we inquired and learned they pay by the ton. A *ton* of chamomile blossoms? My Cornell Ph.D. suddenly seemed useful. Once we got a roof over our head, it was time to scrub nails and go look for jobs. We paid cash for these acres and the building materials, from money saved while working in New Hampshire. Living off the grid, growing our own food, we figured on earning just enough to cover taxes, phone, and car.

It takes two people, not two incomes, to keep this homestead going, especially back then. Two to fill the kerosene lamps and trim the wicks, split wood, stoke the fire, and cook from scratch. And in summer, of course, the garden. Then came Noah. Nothing is less simple than the simple life when you add a baby, though a one-room house did make it easy to watch him. Watch him...watch him...all day long. Haul water while he naps. Wring out stinky diapers for trips to the laundromat. Hang them on the line to dry. Teaching started to sound pretty good. Part-time, at night, at the University of Maine. And Kal took a part-time job in the day as a nursing-home social worker. We became a dual household, two half-jobs, one small income.

The students who called are on their way here, so I'll take a break from weeding to start some soup for them. I light the gas under a kettle of lentils, throw in a whole onion, hot pepper, and bay leaf. I still don't take this gas burner for granted. Our first cookstove burned wood only, short logs, loaded from the top. My arms grew strong moving a heavy canner filled with boiling jars just to throw in more wood. After eleven years of this, we replaced the Stanley with a refurbished 1912 cookstove, pretty curves, beige enamel finish with chrome trim, and the name "Dual Household" embossed on the oven door. "Dual" because the left side is a wood cookstove with a big fire box, and for quicker cooking or canning the right side has four gas burners. The oven heats with either fuel.

We take our dual-fuel stove's motto to heart. Two people run this household, and this household runs two people. Like "Dual Household," we are powered by wood and gas. Grounded by the wild woods we call home, we burn another form of gas to drive off to town. We never knew, when we came here to tread lightly on the earth, that our choices would dance the line between help and harm. Life choices are not as simple as weeding in the garden, where it's clear what goes, what stays. Unforeseen complications, the balance of cost and benefit keep us always weighing our actions. When the students get here, filled with why-do-you, how-do-you questions, my belief in the choices we've made will be confirmed. They stand on the brink of adulthood with few people to show them alternative ways to live. If I'd stayed in the woods and not gone into the world, they would not have me to ask. So I burn gas, and hope my work has some redeeming value to the earth. I stir the simmering lentils and run my hand over the motto on the oven door before heading back to the garden. The stove keeps reminding me that life on earth is one big dual household, as we each struggle to blend with or control what we are bound to.

Down on my knees again with a fresh bucket, I'm weeding and thinking about these students. They are nothing like the ones I taught in my first job at the Augusta branch of the state university, a small campus with two multi-purpose buildings and a vast parking lot for commuting students, mostly older than me, with families and jobs. I taught them, but I should say they taught me—that back-to-the-landers are not the only ones to grow big gardens, haul water, and drive on muddy roads, in case I still thought we invented the idea. Living close to the land is deeply rooted in Maine, and they wrote wonderfully about deer hunting, chopping wood, putting up food just like their parents and grandparents.

After four years of night teaching, I landed a part-time job at Colby College in 1982. The difference between the two jobs was literally night and day. Colby is a private liberal arts college that sits high above Waterville, with a glorious view of the Kennebec River valley. The brick buildings are arranged around quadrangles with rows of shade trees. Granite steps rise up the terraced hillside to a neo-classical library. The athletic facility, when I first saw it, made me cry, and I've never gotten over the contrast between these two schools.

I can make a better living at Colby, and it's just the type of college teaching job I hoped for while in graduate school. So my life became dual in another sense, part homesteader, part professor. Following the rubric of our beloved stove, I built a firewall between life at home and life in the world. Wood and gas don't mix. Ka-BOOM! Keep the professor out of the garden. Keep the homesteader out of the classroom. Keep Route 3 between me and the college.

And speaking of Route 3, I hear a car crunching along our dirt road, and here they are. Kelly and Sarah emerge from a brand-new Saab with Sam and Kaz, each carrying a water bottle and outfitted in high-tech outdoor gear. This generation is born of 'sixties parents, some who stayed on the land, some who got rich in booming times. Either way, those 'sixties values came through in their kids. These twenty-first–century students enjoy their privilege but know some people have nothing, and they want to do something about that. What a change from the fast-lane students of the 1980s, who deemed me "a 'sixties throw-back" when I confessed to reading their papers by kerosene light. If I praised the act of growing food, they would respond, "But why would you want to, when you can go to the supermarket?" Why, they demanded, do I choose to live in the slow lane when I could have wall-to-wall carpeting? I only made matters worse when I told them about our composting toilet, and trips to the laundromat, and—at the time—no refrigerator. They concluded, with a certain disdain, that their professor was living in the breakdown lane.

Had I, in fact, suffered a breakdown? Ph.D. at 25, disillusioned at 26, I'd jumped off the edge of a career when Belknap closed. Maybe I wasn't ready to be a teacher if it meant taming students, fixing their grammar, imposing deadlines, branding them with a grade. I dropped out in the face of Watergate, Vietnam, corporate pollution, a collapsed oil supply. If I gave my days to reining in students' wild side, wouldn't that just make me the tool of all I was running from? Okay, so I broke down. The pines of Belknap called me back to myself. Trees are good at that.

"Wow, is that the garden?" Kaz exclaims, running toward the vast brown rectangle as if she's been cooped up in the library for eighteen years. "Awesome!" She spins with joy, her water bottle flying out of her grip and landing in the grass.

Sam says, "Is this the compost pile you want us to move?" He pushes up the sleeves of his Lacrosse jacket and pulls his hat down over his eyes, ready to work.

"Let's have a tour first." Kelly is brimming with questions—Did you really build all this yourselves? Is that wood pile all you need for heat? Are those solar panels? How do they work?

I chuckle, thinking of the 1980s, and how students didn't want to hear about our new photovoltaic system, or the politics of Jimmy Carter's tax credit that helped us pay for it. They didn't want stories about babies born by natural childbirth who play in the local pond naked and suck home-made popsicles frozen by solar power. Even in a course about gender, they didn't want the observations of a mother who shared all household duties with her husband. They wanted authoritative professors who knew their academic stuff.

"How did you learn to do all this?" asks Sarah. She grew up on a farm in Wisconsin, and shovelled plenty of manure in her day. So she grabs a bucket and starts filling it with compost. Sam joins in, and before long, there's a big dent in the pile as they march two buckets at a time to the far end of the garden. Kelly is still pouring out questions—What vegetables do we grow? How do we preserve them for winter food? Is that a solar food dehydrator over there? Did we build it? Meanwhile, Kaz flits like a butterfly from one end of the garden to another, going "Wow!"

All this makes me smile with pleasure at the external forces that came along to make our choices bloom. I'd weeded academia out of my life after Belknap. Good-bye briefcase, good-bye books, into the bucket with you. I learned to build, garden, preserve food, heat with wood. By the time I returned to the professor thing at Colby, I had so much life to offer, yet my job was to teach writing, literature, critical theory. I was definitely not in the breakdown lane, no matter what the students thought. I was moving forward in the slow lane, creeping along the banks of the mainstream. But I was unable to breach the duality between life in the wild and life in the tame. Even in my home town, I kept the "professor" side quiet. I was known as "one of them hippies come here in the 'sebnties." One day, as the mail carrier dropped an envelope from the wad she was tossing into our rural mailbox, she looked at the address, and then at me standing there in my overalls, and asked, respectfully, "Are you a *real* doctor?" I said no, of course.

It took the Ice Storm of 1998, putting half a million Mainers in the dark for weeks, to bring my pieces together. Overnight we apparently became model citizens with our independent life in a wood-heated, solar electric home. Even the news media took notice. Next came the Y2K scare, for which we were well prepared with power, water, heat, and a cellar full of potatoes. On New Year's Eve we watched the digits spin, thinking we'd finally hit the payoff for choosing an alternative life. 2-0-0-0. Nothing happened. False alarm for the apocalypse. This time. Then came 2001, and the world had its eyes opened by terrorist attacks, mad cow disease, tainted spinach, bird flu, and a repeat of what threw Kal and me into this life in the first place—threatened oil supply, inflation and debt, pollution, scandal, another war. Before we knew it, lo! we were *chic* with our organic and very local food that demands nothing but peanut butter snacks to fuel its transport, by us, in a garden basket, from farm to kitchen. Students now know me as a tree-hugger and vegetable advocate who also teaches English. Wait long enough and even "simple living" comes back into style.

"It's so quiet here," sighs Kaz, finished spinning and flitting, and taking up a shovel now. "I'd love to live like this."

"But what about your iPod, Kaz? Could you live without that?" teases Sam.

"You could still have an iPod," I say, wrestling a few more buckets out of the jammed tool shed. "You can have whatever you want. It's about making your own choices, and not just going along with whatever's expected."

"Remember Thoreau," says Sarah, stopping to tie her bandanna.

"Aww, he probably had a cell phone in his satchel," says Sam.

"No, I mean the way he questioned how 'the mass of men' lived, and didn't feel stuck with those choices."

"'Lives of quiet desperation,'" Kaz mutters sadly.

"See, if he'd had a cell phone..."

"I can just hear him, saying, 'Hello, I wish to speak a word for Nature,'" laughs Sarah.

"Luckily, Nature never hangs up," says Sam.

"Hey, Professor," calls Kelly from behind the barn, "where does this path lead?"

"Into the woods. Let's go!"

Kelly crashes ahead of us up the woods road, if you can call it a road. Trees crowd both sides of a narrow green stretch of no trees. And it only stays like this because we pluck little pine and spruce seedlings from the path. A good case of how choice leaves a mark. I often complain about the strictly controlled landscape at the college. The paths are asphalt. Each tree has a circle of bark mulch. Autumn leaves get sucked up and trucked away. But I admit that the difference between the campus and our tended yard is only a matter of degree. I can't claim to share Thoreau's view of landscaping—"hope and the future for me are not in lawns and cultivated fields...but in the impervious and quaking swamps"—or why would I spend my days dragging the bucket around? How do I reconcile our turf battle with resident insects and animals, with the view of "man as an inhabitant, or a part and parcel of Nature"?

It was teaching Thoreau in a course called Land and Language that helped me heal the split between wild and tame in my dual life. Trying to keep two separate lives meant bringing only half of me to each. What powers me is the friction between these two lives, and having to bridge the contradictions. No wonder Thoreau chose to live "a border life" at Walden Pond, so close to the village. The contrast allowed him to discern what was truly essential to life. Teaching Thoreau and, like him, writing about this so-called simple life, allowed a new voice to seep into both my lives. I soon discovered that in a small town, a professor who hauls water will be listened to at town meeting. At the college, where nothing is real until it's in a book, I'm finally authorized to speak about life on the land. And not just to speak and write about it, but to grapple with this niggling question of what belongs and what is imposed, what is wild and what is tame.

"Stop when you get to the bridge," I call to Kelly and Kaz, who are out of sight now. Sarah trails behind studying moss.

"This place is wild," says Sam, peering into the dense woods. "No one made this grow. Not like your garden."

"True, but it's still rain and sun that make the vegetables thrive. There's only so much a person can do. Plants have their own reasons."

"Why do you think plants just try to reproduce, while humans want so much more?"

"I guess we like to think we're in control. We want to choose."

"Sometimes I wish I didn't have to think so much," he sighs.

Kaz comes running toward us. "That bridge is way cool. Hurry up, Sam. You have to see this." She leads the way to the little stone bridge, where Kelly is marching across and back, across and back.

"The bridge is choice," Sam says. "Walk one way, turn around, walk the other. The stream stays the same."

"Not according to Heraclitus," says Kaz the philosophy major. "He said you can't put your finger into the same river twice."

"But the bridge is always there," I say. "Choice is always there for us two-legged types, right, Sam? What's okay, what's not okay. The trick is not to believe one way is the only way. To walk in balance over the swirling stream, and back again."

"Yeah, and not fall off."

"Maybe the stream is like the way everything is always changing," says Sarah, catching up to us, "like with technology, always forging ahead. It's not good or bad. It just is."

"We wouldn't be here without technology," I concur. "This bridge wouldn't be here. This path wouldn't be. Any time we use a tool that extends our reach—a hoe, a bucket—it's technology. So I can't very well wish for no technology..."

"But Professor," pleads Kaz, "I love my computer!"

"I just don't like the way some tools have the power to reach right into my life and make me go fast when I want to go slow."

"But how did your students contact you before e-mail?"

"They came to my office hours on campus, Kelly. And when I was home, I was home. I like those kind of boundaries. But, I hate to admit, the Internet is teaching me nature's lesson: control is an illusion. Everything follows its own rules. The Internet is wild. It erases the lines I used to work so hard to maintain. I can be home on a Sunday, burning brush in the rain, and without even taking off my boots I can come inside and answer your e-mailed question, then go out again to the glowing embers. I can read your draft and send back comments during a raging blizzard that buries my car in the driveway."

"The Internet is wild?" repeats Sam. "What a crazy concept! That something so civilized, so technologically advanced, is actually wild, the way it grows at its own pace and spreads information unpredictably."

"Maybe everything is wild except our attempts to decide what isn't," reasons Sarah.

"Great idea," I say. Students so often give me the answer I've been struggling toward. "Only the line is tame. I like that. Not the fiber-optic line, but the line that says this is okay, this isn't." I glance up at the maples who watched me fall off the bridge that time in my zeal for putting nature ahead of technology—the roaring stream drowning out the chainsaw noise. "And that's the very line that can make us so unhappy. Complaining about change, trying to stop it."

"Nature is change," Kelly chants as she crosses the bridge over the burbling stream. "Change is nature," she says, turning back toward us.

"Hey, shouldn't we get back to the compost pile? We were almost done," urges Sarah.

"And after we finish, I have some lentil soup for us."

"Race ya," yells Kaz as she and Sam take off.

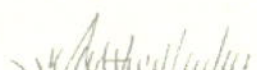

Back home, they keep hauling compost from the shrinking pile to the garden beds, while I start on another grassy edge. I love this May work. It helps me recover from the academic year that's just coming to its bruising finish. The students' shrieks and laughter as they carry buckets show how they, too, need the garden's wildness to heal from the civilizing work we perform with so many words. Wait, did I say the garden's wildness? All this time I've been contending that weeds are the wild thing as I plunk them into the bucket to tame the garden. These definitions are turning into each other. My knees know the edge as I straddle the line, but which side is wild? Or is it, as Sarah proposed, only the edge that's tame?

There wouldn't be much point to gardening, or to teaching, if the cultivated didn't turn around and become wild. All through June, amid swarming black flies and mosquitoes, Kal and I will don bug nets and continue to pluck every growing thing from the soil except our chosen plants. By mid-July, bean rows will merge to become a crowd of leaves, runners, and blossoms moving in unison to the rhythm of the breeze. The pumpkin plant will propel itself by powerful tendrils toward the beans. Corn will send up tassles whose scent brings on the pollinating bees. By August, few patches of the sustaining brown earth will remain. Green ripens to yellow, orange, and red, all on its own. If the tamed did not exceed the tamer and do its wild thing, we would have nothing to can in the fall.

While the tomatoes are turning red in September, I'll be heading back to a new class of freshmen, docile like tender spring plants. Teaching, too, is a dance along the edge of tame and wild. I'll spend hours with a pen poised above their papers, nurturing the creative spark while correcting commas. By October break, after students go back home for a visit, their college roots will have taken hold and they'll become bold. November, with the lure of Thanksgiving to distract them, will make them go wild. They'll exceed my ability to teach them anything new. In December they'll be ripe, and I'll be ready to can them for sure. I've gotten over the fear of taming their wild side right out of existence. That isn't the point of education. They'll go off into the next semester of their life, obeying their own rules if what we call taming has had its desired effect.

I stand up and slap dust off my jeans. I lug the weeds up the gentle slope and dump them in a pile where they'll slowly become compost, a wild process that allows them to be spread again on the tame side of the line, to help the pampered plants go wild. "That looks great!" I say, stepping over an electric fence that circles the section of garden the students have dressed with finished compost, last year's weeds. "Want lunch?"

They drop their shovels and follow me past blueberry bushes under an arch of bird-proof netting, and a raspberry patch protected from porcupines by a high chicken-wire fence. "Boy, you sure have a lot of fences!" observes Sam.

"Yeah, and plants just go their merry way inside and outside these borders. The line's the only tame thing, as Sarah said, and it's a permeable barrier with life on either side."

"Life is the main thing," says Kaz. "Everything has its opposite—and it all adds up to one."

We go inside where "Dual Household" has our lunch all ready.

Sarah ladles up five bowls, and we carry them to the screen porch. From the wicker chairs we watch, unbothered, a teeming world of insects who want us for lunch. Nature itself is a dual household. Everyone eats everything even if we erect a barrier with a door that slams. The line is clear, but for all our human effort, the wild and the tame call both sides home.

Holy Kitchen

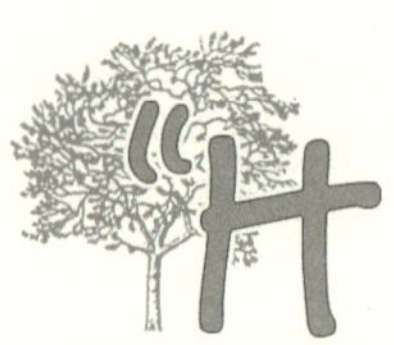

"Has anyone spoken for the pears?" The couple stares at me from the cluttered kitchen table, where at 7 a.m. they're taking a break from early morning farm work. I guess I have it easy, commuting to a college where I'll sit at a desk, stand in front of a blackboard, talk, listen, read, write. But I know how bone-tired and gritty they feel, no choice about what to do because of one choice they made years ago, to live on the land and adhere to the liturgy of its demands. For them, it's cows. For me it's fruit and vegetables that run my life when I'm not taking time off to teach or grade papers.

"They're yours," says the woman I've come to call the Pear Lady. (She doesn't like that title. "I'm no lady," she demurs.) "Too busy for canning."

I've been stopping here for ten years, but she and I go back a hundred years, when her abundant pear tree was just a spindly sapling planted in the dooryard of a Maine farm. Back before the barn held cows milked for the upscale organic market, or sometimes no cows at all in a lagging economy. Back when all cows were organic, and barns were always full, and horses pulling wagons clopped by on a dirt road.

I clop by in a station wagon two days a week. I always noticed the farmhouse, a two-story place with crumbling shingles and plastic-covered windows, tractors and balers and trucks in the dusty driveway. A bed of colorful, hastily tended perennials and a little stand with bouquets for sale. I never even noticed the tree in front of the gaping dark barn. One warm September afternoon the sun hit the tree just right, and I slammed on the brakes—just look at those yellow pears! I picked my way across the mucky yard in my good shoes, but the owners were in the milk room where the *chug-chug-chug-chug* of the pump blotted out my "Hello-o!" So I left a note on the manure-crusted doormat of the house, where assorted kittens crowded around a small bowl.

And now, one day every September, I stop by in the morning to ask, and return on the way home to fill up some bags while the Pear Lady who's not a lady chats with me about why the tree bears so well. Neglect, she claims, and being fertilized by rotting pears. Nothing is wasted. She warns me away from wasps who gorge on fallen fruit. She warns her husband away, too, as he rounds the side of the barn with his mower. "He'd've mowed right over these pears if you hadn't come today," she clucks. He'll be happy, though, when I leave a jar of pear nectar on the step next time I drive by.

We have a one-day-a-year relationship, after which I take an alternate route to work, because there are still pears on the tree and I always have more jars, and I just can't help myself. I say we go way back even though ten years is only a tenth of the pear tree's age. Stooping for the yellow fruit, talking about canning and our sons and the weather, we are two women whose friendship is rooted in a tree.

Why don't I plant one of my own, she asks after a few years of our annual ritual. So we do. Two, in fact. Their beautiful goblet shape foams with white blossoms every spring. We prune them, feed them, weed them, squish bugs and wrap the trunks against mice for the winter. But so far, not a single pear. Neglect, she said? We don't do neglect at our place. Maybe, despite our busy lives, we aren't busy enough, not like the Pear Lady who stops to chat just once a year when the professor with the dirty knees comes by.

I hope by the time I retire and stop commuting past her farm, I'll be crawling around under our two trees picking up fallen fruit. Maybe she'll be retired, too, fulfilling her dream of making dried-flower wreaths, while her son milks the cows and mows the fields. But the pears won't taste the same without the lady who's not a lady standing by. Ritual and relationship—them's the roots.

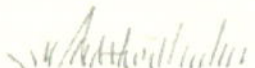

To the kitchen, then, pears spilling out of grocery bags, clean jars lined up on the counter. But the pears aren't quite ready, even though today I have time for them and tomorrow I'll be busy grading a stack of papers. I go outside to the ripening garden and return with a great snowy head of cauliflower. The kitchen is a place of transformation, where nature merges with civilization. Waist pressed against the well-worn maple counter, I am anchored at the edge, where I belong.

In the garden, a pocket knife initiated the move from the natural pole to the civilized as I sliced through the cauliflower's woody stalk. The basket, artfully woven from strips of ash wood, provided the container for nature's bounty. We're a hybrid unit, the cauliflower, the pocket knife, the basket, and I, and back to the kitchen we go.

The cut stalk bleeds when I lift the cauliflower from the basket. I tear off green leaves and drop them into a stainless steel compost tray, metallic pit-stop on the way back to soil. The head is alive. The weight of it fills both hands, and I caress its brain as it lands on the counter. This cauliflower thinks. This cauliflower feels. I stick the point of the kitchen knife in among a complex of white stalks and separate the flowerets, each a miniature replica of the whole.

Cauliflower might have seemed the perfect finger food for a baby when my mother once placed it on my high-chair tray, but I remember wailing, "No-o-o, it's calling me! It said my name!" She tried broccoli, thinking call-i-flower might have confused me. Again I refused. "Treeeees, it's treees," I cried. The miniature world is full-scale to a child. Vegetables are trees, powerful gods of light. A bright green tree lying on its side is not food, even if it is on her plate.

Now I know that eating brings the outside inside, into the house, into the body, so really it's all one side. The endless interface carries people through history, a baby girl banging on her tray, in love with trees, and a woman in her kitchen listening to the intricate thoughts of cauliflower. I dismember its cells with knife, steam, and teeth. Its juice becomes my juice. Its energy gives me strength to grip the knife that transforms it. It calls my name. I am cauliflower.

At the moment in history when we arrived at our place in Maine, we found the scattered remnants of the old settlers' kitchen. A rusted knife, the lid of a crock, blue Mason jars, broken plates and cups reminded us that the first mission of life is to eat. Everywhere a tangle of plants grew without help from us two hippies and our books about organic gardening. If we'd never tilled the rocky soil to cultivate our chosen vegetables and fruits, we still could have feasted on wild blueberries, apples, dandelion greens, burdock roots, raspberries. Like the Sukeforth family of 1777, we haul crops into the kitchen and transform them into food. Peel and chop, cook and eat—potatoes, onions, corn. We insert a kitchen between us and the land, and tunnel our share of the abundance through mouth and gut on its way back to soil. Wielding a knife, we step into the cycle, partners in a porous dance with plants. Plant-body becomes our body, their oxygen becomes our breath, our carbon dioxide is theirs. Eventually, we will be eaten by what we ate. The body returns to soil. We move through the land and it moves through us.

In the kitchen, a rhythmic sense of time prevails. Seasons lap up against the windows, and with them, waves of produce beginning with greens, moving on to peas and strawberries, beans and broccoli, pears and peaches and tomatoes, then trailing off into cabbage, pumpkins, kale. You do what they demand to avoid drowning in yield, and the next thing you know it's winter and your labor pays off. The food keeps the body warm so it can keep the kitchen warm one stick of wood at a time.

Or the kitchen might be a still-life, telling no time at all, if it's abandoned like the one I found in Tuftonboro, New Hampshire in 1973, where I stood on the porch and pressed my nose against the wavy windowpane with longing. Old canning jars sat on the table, a black iron sink where no water had run for decades, while on my side of the window, presidents were assassinated, driven from office, replaced, and the Vietnam War raged on. I set time in motion inside the glass when I imagined a woman at the sink washing jars, a jelly-bag of cooked grapes dripping into a kettle. She measures out sugar, she stirs with a wooden spoon, all done just so, the same every year. Sealed jars cool on the table by the window, glowing purple in the haze of my breath on the pane.

A kitchen is not a vacuum-sealed jar, much as I wanted to hold the twentieth century out by converting to the religion of canning. History leaks into the kitchen through the radio. Tragic news comes to stand beside you when least expected. With a pregnant belly between me and the counter in March 1979, I'm planting a flat of tomato seeds when I hear about the explosion at Three Mile Island. My hands keep dropping seeds into tiny furrows while nuclear fallout drifts over the countryside. The baby somersaults inside me. In June 1989, my ten-year-old Noah lays long red stalks of rhubarb on the pink-stained chopping block for me to slice, when news comes that Chinese student protesters have been shot in Tiananmen Square. The pie goes in the oven. The students die. In January 1991, I'm scrubbing scalloped potatoes from a baking dish in sudsy water when Kal yells from the living room, "They're bombing Baghdad!" and I rush to the TV as a thousand points of deadly light fall upon Iraq. The crusty casserole sits soaking. And there's more to come, worse and worse, while our hands stay busy with daily chores.

Thus the allure of canning, by which you seal out change. Peaches will float in honey syrup as long as the vacuum holds, no matter how complicated the world becomes. Sometime in the future, sun-sweetened fruit and the nectar of long-gone flowers will feed our older selves, for we can't avoid aging though the peaches stay forever ripe. I'm captivated by the glimpse of eternity inside those glass walls.

So captivated that I let peaches rule me on this muggy afternoon. The pears safely made their journey from tree to jars, and down the stairs to a cellar shelf. These late peaches are an unexpected gift, all because my neighbor came by with a carton of empty jars, offering me a more burdensome eternity—will I never finish, will I forever be washing and filling jars, will winter never come to save me from myself? He doesn't know I can't stop till all the jars are full. Waste is something I just can't condone. So off to my friend Don's peach tree, and now I'm lying on the cool kitchen floor, windows closed to keep out the heat, wondering why I need peaches after all. I roll over and study the dust under the stove. My feet are hot. I want to lie here forever. On the counter, peaches tower over me, demanding obeisance: Light the burner! Get this still-life moving!

But what is waste, really, if we all trend downward to the earth where our life will be food for other lives? Fruits drop to the ground to feed worms and ants and wasps and skunks. Or, suspended in glass, they get swallowed later. Pears, peaches, tomatoes, they're all headed for compost whether they run through us or not. I think I'll just lie here a little while longer.

And now my grandmothers, seeing me immobile on the floor, join the nagging peaches. *Eat, eat!* You never know when Cossacks might ride horses through the barley and plunder the apricot trees. *Oy!* Did we suffer in steerage, headed for the promised land with nothing but a heel of pumpernickel and a dill pickle, so you could let such peaches go to waste?

Okay, okay, I'm getting up already. Next year there might be no fruit, which is the line Kal always chants. His immigrant soul argues for putting up whatever we get our hands on, no matter how many full jars rest on the shelves. For my part, I sing the praise of work and reward, canning so I can keep on canning, eating to keep on eating. In the words of my grandfathers, *L'chaim!* To life!

I raise myself up on one elbow. The peaches eye me with impatience. Outside, not a leaf stirs in the blazing heat. Lighting the burner will commit me to attendance at the afternoon service, but before I dip into this abundance, I regret those pints of green tomato chutney sitting below me in the cellar since 1977. I wasted my time because I didn't want to waste the tomatoes. And now those poor tomatoes have wasted more than a quarter-century waiting their return to the promised land.

Outside their vacuum, time marched on, in our little life as well as in the wider world. The last thing those tomatoes remember is the dim light of kerosene lamps, the splash of hand-carried water poured from a jug. While they wait in the dark cellar which didn't even have a finished house on top of it, we added a bedroom, a living room, solar electricity, and a water pump. While chutney mellows in syrup with raisins and ginger, half my adult life has passed, and I still don't like green tomato chutney.

But these luscious peaches need not fear the limbo of the uneaten. I am a peach-crazed woman, on my feet now, scalding the fruits in hot water, peeling away the fuzzy skin. Slice them in half, pit them, save one pit for each jar as a farm woman once told me (for flavor, she said, and a reminder that peaches come from trees). Fit them prettily into jars, fill with honey syrup, process in a steaming canner, remove to the counter at the ding of a bell. The jars seal—*pop!*—marking the moment not of peaches' death, but of their still-life inside sterile glass. When I pry up the lid next winter—*pfffffft!*—peaches will magically re-enter the land of the living where I grow older thanks to them.

Older and older, enmeshed in a liturgy some call doing the chores. The seasons set these psalms to music and take us through the days. At first it required mental effort, trial and error. We often stepped on each other's toes. But after thirty years, moves that seemed like so many rules have become a meditation. The prayer book—jokingly dubbed "Manual for the Operation of Kal and Linda's Place"—tells us what to do when. Garden calendar, annotated list of crop successes and failures, schedule for painting the window trim, instructions for maintenance jobs like emptying the composting toilet or changing the generator oil. At the autumn equinox, raise the angle of the solar panels to catch the winter rays. Spring equinox, lower the angle. We keep track of everything in case one of us dies, we say. In case someone else has to run the place if we decide to take a vacation. In case we sell to a young couple such as we were, on our hopeful trip to West Virginia in search of a farm. Or maybe Noah will take over someday. The records tell the history of our blessed struggle to manage a fertile place that loves us but doesn't much care if it grows milkweed or eggplant.

But sometimes the extraordinary happens, and jotting it in a notebook just isn't enough. That's why I'm collecting a stash of gold coins on a shelf in the cellar. Great big gold coins the size of canning jar lids. In fact they are canning lids, each one marked with a date: "9-11-01." Future archaeologists may wonder why the other jar lids from that year say only "01." Why these dated ones, saved in a special place, as if hoarded for a rainy day?

It wasn't rainy on September 11, 2001, but a perfect fall morning. Kal had gone off to work in town, and I was alone with the dawn sun slanting across a basket of tomatoes, filling the kitchen with a harvest-red glow. I sharpen the knife, line up sparkling Mason jars, and plunk lids into hot water. I am so happy to be quartering red tomatoes and packing them in jars, that the hissing canner is all the music I want. Who needs the radio?

By 9:30, the first load is ready to process. The phone rings. I wipe my hands and turn the flame down under the canner. I already know it's Anna calling from Washington, D.C. We have an appointment to edit an essay. When I answer, she's breathless. "Have you heard what's happening in New York City?" My heart lurches. Noah just left for a job in New York after a summer helping us grow these peaceful tomatoes. She tells me. The World Trade Center. Two planes. Has to be terrorism.

Already I'm turning like a sunflower toward the living room, the television, the map of Manhattan. "What do you want to do?" I ask. "Shall we hang up?"

"Let's just do it," she says.

It's hard to believe we put our instincts on hold and let work seal us off from the rest of the world. In those minutes, we miss the news of the Pentagon, the Pennsylvania plane crash. Anna doesn't know her co-workers are being evacuated. As soon as we hang up, she flees her empty building in a panic. I streak to the TV in time to see the towers collapse, people race away from the black cloud swallowing lower Manhattan. Broadway. My fingertips go cold on the buttons of the remote. Our son works on Broadway. I hear my voice shout "NOAH!" His name bounces off the quiet of the house, and that's when I remember the tomatoes.

Back in the kitchen, full baskets wait in the sunny window. The canner hisses gently. I shut off the burner. Turn on the radio. Pick up the phone. New York does not even ring. Run back to the television. Meanwhile, the sunlight moves along its usual slow path across the floor.

I watch them shouting and running and choking. *Noah, my Noah!* Finally I run outside where crickets are chirping. Tear into the woods and crash under two tall pines. I don't know it yet, but in Brooklyn Noah is emerging from the stalled subway, walking miles back to his apartment, calling us to leave a message, "I'm okay, I made it home." Which helps but doesn't erase the horrors still playing on TV when I return from the woods. I resume canning, this time with radio on. I don't want to be the fool, obliviously cutting up tomatoes while the world comes falling down. The solace of finished jars cooling on the counter keeps me from imploding.

An archaeologist, picking through the remains of our cellar a hundred years from now, will recognize the date on these lids as no ordinary September day. Innocent jars of garden tomatoes say nothing of history, unless I mark them "9-11-01." I am a witness, these numerals say, I am a survivor. But all through the afternoon, every hot jar I lift from the steaming canner cools my faith in the future. This day proves that fragile glass is no match for history. The seal that kept me safe—this reclusive and self-reliant life—is broken. Now I wonder, will we be hiding down cellar along with these tomatoes, eating them one cold jar at a time, just to stay alive? And if so, will I even want to live?

Yellow, orange, red...the harvest goes on. Tomatoes pass through these colors on the way to maturity. But as America comes together and falls apart, the color-coded alerts make me wonder whether we've matured as a nation. If our shock and grief lead only to surveillance and defense, we're still green tomatoes on the vine. The passage through yellow, orange, and red, through fear and anger to heartfelt wisdom, yields a more difficult crop: the understanding that all people want the same thing. Home and land, and the security to sit down to a meal, and watch our children grow. We're all tied to the same necessities, and until we embrace that wisdom, we'll never be safe. No kitchen can hold out history, and ingesting home-grown tomatoes even with a blessing on our lips can't save us from consequences. There's a food chain in geopolitics, too, and we will be eaten by what we ate.

But hope is local. Hope is internal. And internal becomes external in nature's inside-out dance. All the tomatoes come in before frost, meet with the heat of canning, go down to the cold cellar, come up to join garlic and onion in hot olive oil, cool off on the pasta, go down into a warm belly and eventually back out to the cold. As winter progresses, I save the lids from the 9-11 jars to bolster hope. The growing stack tells me, "Right now you're okay. You are alive. This is your life." Nature keeps us present, to learn from the trials of history. We harvest. We eat. We survive. These lids redeem my faith in life, one gold coin at a time.

The real gold is black, what gardeners call "black gold." If ever your faith needs boosting, just stick your arm into a working compost heap and feel the deep warmth of grass clippings melding with dry leaves. They all get along, unlike the peoples of the world, producing vital heat and the resource to grow more grass, more leaves, always more.

Compost happens. Every cornstalk and tomato vine, rotten melon and broccoli gone to flower, is tossed on the pile. The many become the one as worms move through the dark pile propelled by their eating. All diversity shares a common destiny in this holy kitchen where heat comes from within. In spring, the finished compost will enrich the garden as we move through our rituals propelled by our eating.

The end is the beginning. A sealed canning jar only presents the story of an afternoon preserved in its tracks. It's not eternity you're glimpsing through the glass, but the illusion that peaches in honey can last forever. The globe keeps turning. Eternity is matter on the move, out here, on this side of the glass.

Eat Kale and Pray to Your God

i

The black coffee warms my face as I peer into the buttercups and roses of my mother's Spode. Steam dances over the coffee like the snow outside whirling and luffing between buildings at this elder community disguised as a French provincial manor. Snow billows down around the main entrance like a veil that keeps the residents inside. Those menacing icicles are something the architects did not plan on, I'm sure.

Nestled in my father's chair, I'm holding the cup's warmth to my heart. This is the last sip from my mother's Spode. I'm here in Rochester to help Mom pull apart this house of cards. Lampshades and pillows and paintings will crash down around us at the first tug. She'd be happy if all her things just blew away. Not me. It was bad enough, two years ago, seeing the little Mexican chair emerge from a truck in my driveway in Maine, the one I sat on as a child to watch trees dance in a rainstorm. I'd still be able to drink from the old cups here at their new apartment. But now they're finished with things, and we three sisters are suddenly responsible for dispersing their possessions. Where is "home" once everything is scattered?

Dad's not even here. He fell out of bed and broke his thumb last week, while my older sister Joanie was sleeping downstairs in the guest room provided by the management. Mom didn't want to wake her in the middle of the night, didn't want to push the help buzzer either. Dialed 911 instead, and the ambulance took Dad away. When Joanie came up for breakfast, Mom did not know where he was. Joanie retrieved him from the hospital, with a cast on his thumb and bars for the bed. Should have had an aide, too, but our mother, wasting away from chemotherapy worse than the lymphoma it means to cure, was fierce in her refusal of help.

Now Dad has fallen again, trying to put on his slippers. He landed on his back like a turtle and couldn't get up. Again, 911 so as not to bother anyone downstairs. The emergency crew carried Dad out on a stretcher with one slipper on. Mom worked herself into a frenzy because she didn't know where they took him, and he'd gone off without his wallet.

I'm the baby, not used to taking charge in the family, but it's my turn. So much for our special New Year's Eve in Maine, 2000 turning to 2001. We planned to drink champagne and trudge through the snowy orchard singing to the trees, a family tradition. But instead, I came here with a mission: to tame my crazed mother, to find Dad and bring him his wallet. And now, it seems, to oversee the end of home.

"Home is no place for a 91-year-old man with a sick wife," said the doctor where I found Dad, at Strong Memorial Hospital. Dad gripped my hand and begged me to get him out of this prison. "Two falls and we keep him here, unless you hire a 'round-the-clock aide." Of course Mom, all 80 pounds of her, face white as snow, cracked lips, no hair, again said no. So they released him to the Jewish Home, right next door to their independent-living complex. She's too sick to go visit alone in the blustery cold, too confused to take care of herself. We've concluded that she belongs in the nursing home, too.

So I'm curled up in Dad's vacant chair on the last morning of the twentieth century. There's so much to do. Fill out the papers to get Mom on the waiting list. Sort through their stuff which, in the somber snow-light of dawn, looks like as much as they ever had. I can't start without Mom, but she's still in bed. She's always in bed. Chemo-*therapy* they call it? It's killing her. The Spode buttercups and roses are comforting. I put my nose into the empty cup and sniff the coffee residue. Oh, I just want to drown in these buttercups. Want to crawl around on the rug and build little doll houses under the dining room table—there it is, same one I grew up with—and sit on the couch with a storybook propped on that needlepoint pillow my grandmother made. Go sledding and come in for cocoa. Want my happy childhood back. The old man in the nursing home next door, the sick woman in the next room, put us at the center of their life. Now it's up to me to tear it all down.

Those ungodly icicles hold my attention until Mom finally shuffles into the living room and flicks on the light, blasts me out of my rêverie by cranking the thermostat up till the hot air blows my hair. "Are you cold?" she asks. (This means "I am cold" in a language where she never says what she needs.) "No, Ma," I say, peeling off my socks and heading for the kitchen to cool my face with a damp dish towel. Dump the coffee grounds, put the cup and saucer in the sink. Note stacks of white boxes in the refrigerator with uneaten egg salad sandwiches delivered from the dining room, one per day. "Okay," I say, rolling up my sleeves, "want to get started?"

Mom slumps down at the table she'd picked out as a bride and starts counting out pills, doing it wrong. "No, Mom, a pink one every other day."

"What *are* all these?" she lashes out, knocking down the row of bottles, this woman who never got sick her whole life and doesn't believe in medicine. "Why are they torturing me?"

"They're trying to help you, Mom." But I don't believe in medicine either, like mother like daughter. This is torture. She'd decided to quit the chemo last September, after only two rounds. I was here with them, sitting right at this table, when she announced, "I've lived a good 85 years, and I'm ready to die." She hates the new apartment, the pressure to be social after a lifetime of solitary independence. She'd rather die than go down to the elegant dining room every night and sit for two hours with strangers. Barely audible, Dad replied, "I would miss you"—among the few words of affection he's uttered in sixty years of steadily loving his wife, and they swayed her. "I can't just leave him like that," she confided later. "That would be a dirty trick."

As the chemo made her worse, Dad must have come to think it was a dirty trick to entice her to live just for his sake. He must have decided it was time for him to leave. Falling softly on the new carpet, he figured the way out was down. But by now he sees it's not a straight shot to the exit.

"Ready to start?" Mom's got her bald head propped up by elbows on the table. I've already gone through Dad's clothes, miles of suits on a closet rack, a forest of ties, crisp shirts in plastic bags. I packed a shopping bag with what they want him dressed in at the Jewish Home—front-buttoning shirts and sweaters, drawstring pants, underwear and pajamas, and his other slipper. Mom grabs the bag and takes everything out. She fingers the shirts looking for stains, unrolls the socks to see if they're good enough. "He's very fussy, you know, about how he looks." As for herself, she wears the same denim jumper every day, missing one button, and a dirty beige sweater. She has a drawer full of brand-new nightgowns that my oldest sister Barbie buys for her. The hand-woven wool hat I sent is stashed in her closet.

"Why don't we start with the bathroom cupboard?" I suggest, caressing her bald head. Compared to what else has to be done, this is a teacup in a flood. Plastic bottles drop into the trash, soap, detergent, this and that, until we come to the old button basket. She snatches it up with surprising strength and hobbles to the table.

Believe it or not, with the weight of her entire household looming over us, we sit here going over the buttons. The little pearl ones from baby clothes, the extra buttons labelled for items long gone, all the way back to the 1940s. Here's the spare for her denim jumper, and I sew it on, holding the material away from her knees as I stitch. She cradles each button in her chapped hands and tells me about the sweater or dress it goes to, and then says, "Do I still have that?" From time to time, I'm sent to the closet to find out. But of course she doesn't have a silk shirt to her name, and only one sweater.

She's stooped and haggard, with no hair to comb as we get ready for our first visit with Dad next door. Carrying the satchel of his clothes over the handle of her walker, she really does look like a bag lady, despite the good black wool coat. Mom was husky and strong, and now she's a husk. When we appear in Dad's room, tears run from the corners of his eyes, this father who never showed emotion but just did what he had to do. He's got my hand and won't let go. Mom wheels into the bathroom, and he quavers, "Mom looks awful." He begs me to take him home. I shake my head slowly, almost hoping he won't notice my answer. How did I get to be the one who says No to my father? Who am I to say he can't go home? I watch his cloudy brown eyes follow my blue ones as they trace no, no.

Dad never believed he'd live from 1909 all the way to the twenty-first century. But here we are. I kiss his dry lips and wish him happy new year. They're both crying as we leave the room. I'm just trying to steer Mom and her walker past linen bins that reek of urine, focussing my eyes on the Judaic motif printed on the wallpaper, shutting my ears to the demented howls from down the corridor. I am not the little girl in pajamas watching from the stairs as they toast the new year with their friends. I'm not the teen-ager stepping out with a date, all hair-spray and pearly lipstick. I am...what?...the caretaker, the driver, the only one left standing here on the edge of the millennium.

Back at Mom's, the big dining room with teak panelling and Japanese screens is crowded with elegantly dressed residents, some dragging oxygen tanks or pushing walkers. People can't get into this complex if they're on walkers, but it seems they suddenly need them the minute they move in. I'm in a red silk shirt that perked Mom up enough to put on a black turban and turquoise necklace. She actually looks pretty good, despite the chalk-white face.

"Where's Milt?" everyone asks, fishing for a little community gossip. Mom forces a smile and doesn't answer.

"He's in the Jewish Home," I say, coming to her rescue. They're breathless at the titillating prospect of bad news. "Is he coming back?" I picture him going out the door on a stretcher, one slipper on, leaving his home for the last time.

"I don't know," I evade.

"Oh, Harriet," one woman grabs her hand, "you look wonderful. Don't worry, dear, your hair will grow back. Look at me, I survived lymphoma! You can, too!"

Mom crinkles her eyes into crescents, but the second these friendly people turn away, her cheeks go slack. It's hard to explain how a beautiful dining room can be, to someone who wants to die, a torture chamber. She unfolds and re-folds her napkin and looks down at her lap. We wait for the fancy meal we don't even want. Everyone is staring and speculating. I take sips from a water goblet to keep from crying.

Back upstairs after dinner, in the living room with tea, it's almost like old times. Until I present Mom with a pretty tapestry vest I thought she'd like. She blows up. "I can't be the mother you all want me to be! Someone who likes the gifts her daughters pick out, someone who can hold her own with the ladies downstairs!"

"Mom, it's not true. I don't care that you're not like those women." But what is true, and I'm seething with frustration, is that I have a mother who can't accept gifts or help. I find myself yelling back at her, and no dad is here to keep us in check with his commanding "she's your *mother*!" And I don't care if she is. I feel like ripping this red silk shirt to shreds. I rush to the den and grab my nightgown from the suitcase, pull it on and open a book. Move my eyes across the page to steel myself against her sobbing in the other room. This is exactly where we left off in 1965 when I went to college. My I-don't-care-how-you-feel attitude that fit at 18 suddenly shocks me into realizing everything is changed. She is the needy one and I'm in charge here. I get up to go comfort her, and she lunges into me again. I stifle angry retorts until she finally goes to bed, and I'm alone at last.

A little of Dad's scotch, journal propped on Gramma's needlepoint pillow, I scribble my way toward midnight. Kal and Noah...are they wassailing the orchard trees without me? I don't dare call. I don't dare explode. I have to contain myself.

She expects me to sleep in Dad's bed, like last night. But there's no way I'm sleeping in Dad's bed again. I tossed all night, thinking of him falling out and breaking his thumb. She kept getting up and turning the light on, confused about why was I in Dad's bed and where is he? Finally sleep muffled my worries, until the crackling of a cereal box in the kitchen woke me. We got laughing over cereal and banana in the middle of the night, like old times again. But today we laid Dad's strong-box out on his bed, with all those documents and meticulous notes, the weight of it making a huge dent where my father used to sleep. His little world that he kept all locked up was in full view, with no one to tend it now except me and my sisters. Who could ever sleep there after that?

But she insists, coming out of her room at 11 o'clock to turn up the heat. "Come to bed," she orders.

"No, Ma. It's New Year's Eve. I'm staying up to watch the blizzard blow. Look, you can see the blurred outline of those old cottonwoods up on the bank of the Erie Canal. They're holding their own even in this wind. I'm keeping a vigil. I'm watching them watch me through this crack in the blind."

"You always were a little weird about trees," she shakes her head, and goes back to bed. The dark branches against the white sky carry me to midnight. Happy new year, trees. I turn out the light and watch some more. There they are. Here I am. A taut rope of communion anchors me to them in the wild gale that glows yellow-orange from ghostly streetlights. The plow goes by. I feel almost safe as I fall asleep on the couch.

At 3 a.m., Mom comes sailing out of her room in a fury, snaps on the light, and forces me to come sleep in Dad's bed.

"It's too hot in there," I wail. She's standing over me, making me lie down on his bed. Covers me with two afghans, turns up the heat. I'm an abused child, terrified of this crazy mother intoning, "Oh, I'm desperate...desperate..." At last she sleeps and I tiptoe back out to the couch. A cold draft from the window refreshes me, and I watch the cottonwoods for the rest of the night. *Morning will come,* the trees tell me through swirling Lake Ontario snow, *sure it will, shhhhhhhhurrrr...*

New Year's Day. Mom remembers nothing about last night. She is not the mother. I am not the daughter. From now on, I am the aide. The cottonwoods dropped this wisdom on me once I fell asleep in a new millennium that has no meaning to them. They saw a blizzard, a forlorn face peeking between the blinds, two old people sleeping a driveway apart. They witness changes that throw me for a loop, and then summer comes again, and they'll oversee me strolling along the Canal, pressing fingers into the grooves of their trunks, craning my neck to see their glossy heart-shaped leaves swivelling in the breeze. It's all the same to them, and that helps. Let's face it, I couldn't have made it without them, and I mean to thank them by doing what I have to do.

Do I mean the cottonwoods? Or Mom and Dad? I couldn't have made it without them, either. Now it's my turn.

I'm the only passenger on the small plane headed along the Mohawk Valley back to Boston. We fly low over the Catskills, the Hudson River, the Berkshires dusted with snow. The pilot points out Mount Washington's snowy peak off to the left. Down to the right, I spot the unmistakeable shape of the Quabbin Reservoir, and the Pioneer Valley where Noah is by now back at Amherst, walking under giant oaks, in and out of brick buildings, thinking about his senior thesis. I've missed our family millennium celebration. I press my nose to the glass and breathe his name.

*A gentle command bubbles up from my heavy heart and forms steam on the window—*Eat kale and pray to your God. *I close my eyes and see a row of dark green kale calling me home to Maine, where our garden is under snow and fresh kale is just a memory. Even when I open my eyes I still see the kale just the way it glistened in the autumn sun. Powerful enough to hold this plane in the air, strong enough to keep me from suffering an old age like Mom and Dad's.* Eat kale and pray to your God. *I will get old, at home, in the garden, if I can just keep the power of kale in my blood and bones. The power of prayer in my heart.*

ii

This is the first trip back to Rochester with no place to stay. I feel like an orphan, checking into the EconoLodge on Jefferson Road, a typical American franchise strip that was still farmland when I was in high school. With all these steakhouses and malls, I could be anywhere, until I cross the Erie Canal in my rental car and approach the Jewish Home hulking in what used to be cow pasture. I make sure to park within sight of the cottonwoods who saved me last winter. They encourage me with their spring-green leaves.

The accumulation of a life together has shrunk to fit Mom and Dad's room on the fifth floor. The dresser they drove to Buffalo for in 1939 is all that's left. Home no longer exists, if home is furniture and paintings and the chipped dish I once threw on the floor in a tantrum. But Rochester is home, despite all its changes. And home is these two old people who beam when I walk into their room. Home is my willingness to accept what is.

Mom quit the chemo, and miraculously she's getting better, just to spite those doctors. Her new hair grows in unruly white tufts. She still wears the denim jumper. "I just snuck over here and moved in with Dad," she giggles. The whole ordeal of filling out the papers, breaking up the apartment, waiting for a double room, is lost to her, as is the lymphoma. "Oh, I never had anything of the kind," she scoffs. "I only came here to keep Dad company. I guess they can't do anything about it, now that I'm here!"

Dad wanted her company, but now it's a horror show he was too loyal to reveal over the phone. She keeps their room closed tight, and refuses to eat in the dining room with old people in bibs. Their dinner arrives with a knock on the door. When Mom lifts the cover off the tray, she erupts at Dad for daring to have an appetite. "How can you *eat* that? Ugh. It's revolting." If he buzzes for an aide, she shrieks, "I'm your *wife*," and insists on helping him to the bathroom, two old people with walkers. Somehow vehement denial has revived her strength. If she's not careful, she'll get too well for the nursing home, and then where will she be, worldly goods scattered to the winds?

Dad started out here as just an old guy who needed help with his balance. The tireless athlete in him loved the challenge of Rehab. But he kept tipping over, and when his twenty-one days ran out, they moved him to this hopeless floor of moaning patients. He took to his bed in blue pajamas.

Now he's been slipping down into deep slumbers for whole days at a time, while Mom paces back and forth like a caged leopard. I came here this time because it looks like he really is dying. Last week, he tipped over while brushing his teeth and broke some ribs against the handrail. At the hospital, he lost the ability to swallow, but managed to let my sister Barbie know he didn't want a feeding tube. He was ready to die. But not quite. Back at the Jewish Home, he started to swallow again, with difficulty. Now he takes thickened water from a spoon, and puréed dog barf for dinner. I hold his smooth, cool hand as he goes down to sleep, and watch his eyes move under the lids. Hours later, he jerks awake and says, "Did you get your check for the air fare?" but it sounds more like "Dih oo geh yer je...?" It takes me and Mom many tries to interpret. He keeps at it, forcing his lips and tongue to make the sounds, "Did yooo ge yur chec...?"

Barbie, who lives here, is gone to London to help her daughter with a new baby. Joanie and I, both professors, came as soon as spring semester ended. Yesterday, our one day of overlap, we took Dad outside in a wheelchair, Mom with her walker. The massive Jewish Home is wonderfully softened by trees and gardens with benches. We sat under a wisteria arbor, while apple blossom petals drifted down on a warm May breeze. Dad looked vaguely like Dad in a neat plaid shirt and baseball cap. His skinny arms covered with bruises, face stiff with a grimacing smile, didn't hide the "I made it to spring!" joy in his eyes. After gruelling Rochester winters, spring was always his happiest season, with golf and the lawn and the screen porch to look forward to. Joanie and I were already framing the moment as "Dad's Last Happy Day."

Today the head nurse lifts the order for thickened fluids. She kneels down in front of Dad and tells him he can have whatever he wants. "A martini?" she jokes. He looks straight into her eyes and whispers, "Wa...dr." She shows me how to hold a plastic cup to his eager lips. Cold water, the dying man's martini. Later he wakes from a nap and says, "Mmmeer...mmmeeer..." Mirror? Milk? Mom and I lean over him, trying to guess. Ice cream? He nods. I run down the hall for a little cup of vanilla. But that's not it. Again and again, trying to force a plosive sound, "mmmp...mmb...mmbee...mbeer...," beer! My father wants a beer! Labatt's? He nods.

At the nearest store there's no Labatt's so I get something else. A close call in traffic on the way back, my fault. Shaken and exhausted, I lug the beer up to his room. He looks at the label and turns up his nose. I'm furious! Does he want me to risk my life again, just for

Labatt's? Alas, I've failed to satisfy my father's dying wish. He'll just have to drink Corona. And he does, from a plastic cup I hold to his foamy lips. He looks me in the eye as he drinks, the way a nursing baby does. He coughs. The nurse says this is how he will finally die, his lungs slowly filling with aspirated liquid. He might as well have what he wants. And he knows what he wants. For the puréed hot dog under the lid of his dinner tray, he pathetically requests—mustard!

The next day he wakes from a slumber and tries to move his lips, but he can barely talk. He is insistent, grabbing my hand. His mouth forms a question I can't make out. Mom tries. I watch as my little old mother leans over her husband in his bed, a tableau to wrench a heart, made even more poignant by the panorama of Rochester seen from the fifth-floor window behind them like a film of their lives. Bisected by the Erie Canal, the view of their city shows the University of Rochester in the distance, where Dad got his chance to rise from poverty. He and five siblings pooled their resources to pay their widowed mother's rent and put each other through school. Mom, eldest of four, was sent to the U. of R. by her unschooled father, a successful businessman. Just this side of the University, Mt. Hope Cemetery holds the graves of all those grandparents. Closer in, there's Cobbs Hill, known to all our generations as a spot for lovers. Mom and Dad courted there, and later pushed the baby buggy, one, two, three little girls scampering ahead of them around the reservoir. They brought their grandchildren up there, too, tricycles and bicycles and ice cream bars. In the foreground I glimpse the streets they lived on, from one house to the next, slowly moving up in the world.

Against this frieze, I am watching Mom lean closer, trying to understand Dad's question. Finally she gets it. *Is there a threat somewhere?* She repeats his words to be sure, and he nods, his eyes beseeching her so pitifully I can hardly stand to watch. "Oh, *no*," she assures him, tenderly squeezing his forearms and speaking as if to a scared child. "No, we're all as safe as can be," she says like the good mother she was before her identity collapsed and left her to drift into old age with three daughters for ballast. Her voice strengthens with maternal confidence, and she leans right into his face. "We couldn't *be* more safe."

It's September 11, 2001, and I am running down the path into the woods. I scramble up the hill we call Holy Wood, and collapse on the pine needles, televised sounds of Manhattan echoing in my ears. How can it be so quiet here? How can the trees not know, not care? They know. They care. But like the rest of us, they can't do anything about it.

Thank God Dad died in May. Thank God he doesn't have to know about this. He died while 2001 was still a year of hope and promise. He died the morning his youngest grandson, Noah, graduated from Amherst. And now Noah's in Manhattan—oh, what has happened to him?

—IS THERE A THREAT SOMEWHERE?— My God, Dad knew before we knew! He glided out of the present in his deep sleep and saw those two planes heading for New York. Dad! What else did you see?

I get up off the pine needles and race home. What's to become of us? Tell me! I fly through the door and turn up the TV in the living room, the radio in the kitchen. Out to the garden. Dart between rows of vegetables and finally sink to my knees in front of the kale. Kale knows nothing, or everything. I tear off a piece with my teeth, and the dark-green juice opens my throat. DAD! HELP!

iii

"Milton Tatelbaum 1909–2001." Until I see it printed on the memorial cards in a basket by the chapel, I don't quite believe it. I almost believed it at the EconoLodge this morning when Joanie came to breakfast all dressed in black. But disbelief slipped back into place. Finding Mom prim on the edge of her bed in a single room on a different ward failed to convince me that Dad wasn't still on the fifth floor. Three weeks ago, I'd hurried away from him after the ordeal with the beer. I just wanted a beer myself, to tell the truth. Had to get the hell out of that hot, stuffy place. Kissed him good-bye, kissed Mom, and reached for the doorknob. His finger beckoned me, weakly, to come back. He took my hand and wouldn't let go.

Bleary brown eyes, two little buttons sunk into his skull, said he wanted something final, but the man of few words had fewer all the time. I stroked his forehead. "You're doing a good job being old," I said. His eyes gave a self-deprecating flicker, like big deal, what's to be proud of? I wanted to say, the way you're showing me how to accept what is, and bear it. Instead I said, "It's hard being old." His eyes said yes. Then, thinking of how diligently he'd worked to make a secure life for us, I said, "It was hard being young, too." Eyes said no. Last words struggled from his lips, "Mmmaam ookhs mmbeh...r." I agreed. Mom looks better.

She looks so better this morning that she doesn't even look real. Her hair is all grown back, thick and white, and she's gained a little weight. When I go into her room to help her downstairs to the car, to the memorial service, to the reception at Barbie's house with the relatives, she's dressed in a black skirt and white blouse with a stiff collar. She looks like a doll, and I wind her up and guide her walker into the elevator. She doesn't know what hit her. "Where's Dad?" she asks plaintively. "We can't go without *him*."

"Dad died," I have to say. "Remember? You were both in a room on the fifth floor, and now you have your own room on the third floor, and he's gone."

"Gone?"

My finger hits the "L" and we sink to the lobby where a gaggle of old people sits by the front door watching the world go by. We help Mom into the car. "Where are we going? We forgot Dad."

He died in the middle of the night. What she remembers is that he coughed and coughed. What she remembers is that she didn't call the nurse, though I assure her it wouldn't have made a difference. What I wish she did not remember, what I wish I could forget, is that they came and wrapped him in brown paper and took him away to be cremated. In the morning they moved her to the single room.

Really it isn't until after the whole day sitting around at Barbie's eating bagels and lox, until Kal and Noah and I are driving on Jefferson Road and Kal stops on an impulse at the neon "Hot Now!" at Krispy Kreme, that I realize Dad is crispy cremains himself. We step right up to the glass where raw donuts ride along the belt, drop into hot oil, get flipped over to brown the other side, then move under a waterfall of sugar glaze, and roll out hot to the counter. Imagine the horror of watching a cremation through the glass...eyes melt, bones pop, skin crisps. What happens to the teeth? Suddenly the lady hands me a free donut. She must know my father died! And then she hands one to Noah. His grandfather died! Then Kal gets a sample, so light it's like breathing. We're happy, dressed in black and licking our fingers.

The next night we return and hang around where they're handing out free donuts, looking forlorn like our father just died. And we get 'em again! Our mother would not approve, donuts right before bed, donuts at all. Dad would turn over in his grave, if he had a grave and weren't in a little can with his name on it out in the car. Okay, so Dad's cremains are turning over to see us heading in for donuts at this time of night.

"Cremains" is the funeral home's term, and they promised to deliver so we could scatter them in the park. My sisters don't want anything to do with it. But, hey, you don't just let them dump your father in the trash bin. You get the ashes, and you make a ritual, for your own sake if not for his. But the guy from Parsky's Funeral Home never shows up. So we jump in the car, Kal in back, Noah driving, and it's a wild ride under a purple thundercloud about to burst, a daring mission to snatch what's left of my father. I navigate us along the Inner Loop, an expressway that penetrates the heart of the city. It pierces my heart, too, as we pass exit signs for all the old family neighborhoods in reverse chronology, first "East Avenue," where Gramma lived in that elegant glass apartment building after Grampa died, see it over there, behind the spreading copper beech tree? Then at "Culver Road," we glimpse the back of the house Mom grew up in and we visited as kids. There's the fence that kept us from tumbling down onto the trolley tracks that became this speeding expressway. "Park Avenue," now with its hip strip of cafés, then with its tailors and shoemakers and greengrocers, was the neighborhood where Dad and his siblings eventually moved their families to wooden houses with porches and small backyards, where we three were born. Still going backwards in time, here's "Monroe Avenue," where both Mom and Dad's family started out on poorer streets, no porches, patchy yards. There's Mom's high school, and the same run-down shops, some of them now hippie boutiques selling hookahs. "Downtown Rochester" brings us back to the source of all these changes—Dad's career at Sibley's, McCurdy's, Forman's department stores, allowing our family to move to a suburb, many blocks from this Inner Loop.

Racing the darkening cloud, our car probes the innermost loop of family history. We reach "St. Paul Boulevard," where it all began with the scrap metal yard Mom's father owned, providing a solid financial base for all our generations. We exit at St. Paul just as the black cloud bursts open. Through slashing rain and violet lightning, we sail past the original Jewish Home where Dad's father lay for years with Parkinson's, where Gramma's mother sank into toothless old age. And across the street, here at last is the mythic core, the end of the loop—Parsky's Funeral Home. Sooner or later everyone shows up at Parsky's.

Kal and Noah wait in the car while I go into the creepy lavender foyer stencilled with angel wings. Down the corridor I hear organ music from the dim chapel. I remember sitting in there as a bewildered twelve-year-old, at Grampa's funeral, but it wasn't lavender in 1958.

Nothing was lavender in 1958, except the famous lilacs of Highland Park. An oily man in a black suit, the death broker, comes out of the office. "Linda? Right this way."

I sign the release, and take hold of a shiny burgundy shopping bag such as one might walk out of Bergdorf-Goodman's with, containing a small cardboard box, a mini-mini-coffin, labelled "Milton Tatelbaum." Inside there's a gold can, and inside that a plastic bag of gritty ashes with a scorched dog tag, name and number, like what did they do, wire that around his big toe as they pushed him into the oven? (Oh, shades of Auschwitz...how can a Jew choose to be burned?)

The pert little shopping bag seems right for Dad, after a career in women's clothing. "Do with them as you choose," the broker says. Them. The cremains. Not "him." Dad is already dispersed. Is it even legal to scatter ashes in the park? Don't ask. Just take the bag and run. I push open the glass door and carry my dad through the downpour in his shopping bag.

Kal and Noah lean protectively around me as I slide into the passenger seat, slam the door and burst out crying. You can't not know your father is dead when you have him at your feet in a box labelled "Milton Tatelbaum." That label doesn't mean this box belongs to Milton Tatelbaum, like golf clubs or a sweater. This box *contains* Milton Tatelbaum, and I'm in charge of it now. It. Not "him."

My sisters don't want to miss out, so we all head to Highland Park. Joanie's face collapses when Kal opens the can. "Ddaaad?" We each take a plastic cup and sprinkle some giant oaks. Dad liked oaks. Next we sprinkle on a hill with a distant view of the Jewish Home. Just as we finish, a brown rabbit hops out from the bush. "Dad?" says Joanie.

We take the rest of the ashes to Cobbs Hill. Where to put them? Barbie suggests a path into the trees. Here? Then we see a brown rabbit! We sprinkle. Victory lap around the reservoir, ice cream bars from a vendor.

Back at Mom's room, we tell her about the rabbit at Highland Park, the rabbit at Cobbs Hill. She says, with wide blue eyes, "Was it the same rabbit?"

Very late the next night, Kal, Noah, and I pull into our driveway in Maine. A brown rabbit hops across the headlights and disappears under a white lilac bush. We sprinkle the rest of the ashes there the next morning. "What the hell do I want to be in Maine for?" I keep hearing Dad ask. Trust me, you want to be in Maine. I'll watch over you here. You'll watch over me.

iv

"Go help your mother." The budding maple trees speak to me in Dad's voice. From the kitchen window my vision goes to a certain cluster of leaves, but I can't figure out which trunk holds up those branches, which tree is "Dad." I said Kaddish for Dad every night as I walked under them, from May when their tender infant leaves grasped at life, through summer's lush greenery, the red fire of autumn, then bare branches clattering in icy wind. Spring has come around again, a whole year of prayer as I learn to walk alone, a daughter without a father.

"Yitgadal, v'yitkadash sh'mei rabba..." rose from my mouth on molecules of carbon dioxide, and in return for the prayer, the trees bathed me in oxygen. Now Dad's spirit animates the branches, and his voice drops advice on my head.

"Go help your mother." It's so much easier to obey a dead father. So here I sit in a shuttle on the dark runway of Boston's Logan Airport. The tarmac glistens in the spring rain. Planes lumber back and forth, and peppy little fuel trucks, and guys with luminescent wands direct traffic in the night. We sit in the unmoving shuttle, a breathing busful of passengers in limbo. No one talks. A man sticks his head in and calls out a name, and the woman next to me answers, "Here." He tells her the boarding pass she gave him is not valid. He tells her to get off the bus and climb the aluminum stairs in the rain with all her bags and get a new one. He can't guarantee the shuttle will wait for her.

She melts into tears next to me, so close I feel her heat. I can't help myself, I am crying, too. I put my arm around her shoulders. "My mother is dying!" she sobs. "Tonight! She is dying tonight and I *have* to get there!" Her vaporous aura expands and I am encircled by her grief, patting her shoulder, saying, "It's okay. It's okay."

"Let her stay," a passenger yells out. We're all enveloped by her moist aura now, her surging panic. "Yeah, let her stay," says another. Suddenly the shuttle jerks into motion, the agent jumps out, and we drive across the drenched tarmac to our plane. An hour later, we're all marching double-time down the arrival corridor in Rochester, surrounded by Eastman Kodak Company posters of blooming lilacs and smiling University graduates happy in their corporate jobs. We're all in a rush to get there before her mother dies. My mother is not dying tonight, as far as I know. Like a hardy lilac bush chopped to the ground and left for dead, her spindly green shoots have sprung back to life.

"I had lymphoma?" she asks the next morning, sitting on the edge of her bed in the Jewish Home. I run through the story, for the tenth time, of how she got here.

"Yes, you had lymphoma. And Dad fell a few times, so he came here, and then you came, too."

"Did we move here from Edgerton Street?"

"No, Mom. That's the house where us kids were born. You moved here from the Summit." Her puzzled blue eyes have that drowned cornflower look. "The Summit. You know, the elder apartments right next door, see, you have a view of it from your window. You quit the chemo, remember? And they said you only had three months."

"But I didn't die?"

"No. You're right here!"

"I guess I showed them! And you're...Linda? Let's see. You were the youngest. How old are you?"

"I'm 55."

"Noooooh. That can't be right. I'm only 45. And my mother was 94 when she died. So I have another fifty years to live. That seems very long."

"You're 87 now, Mom."

"Oh! I don't feel 87." She giggles like a girl, and reaches to pick up a framed photo of Dad. "This is my husband."

"I know. He's my father."

"Oh!"

"Do you want some tea?"

"Maybe later. Are you cold?" she asks, pulling her ratty beige cardigan tighter. Her bare legs are blue. I'm hot as a boiled beet in the stifling room. Her dry, cool hand reaches for my sweaty one across the tray that holds the nurse's note, "LINDA will arrive TODAY." I think of the woman on the plane, and how grief rose off her like steam, and wonder if she made it to her mother. I don't want my mother to die, but how long until she goes in to lunch and I can leave for an hour?

Mom looks at the Siberian irises I brought, all closed into tight purple fists with bright yellow cuffs. "Those are irises," she declares. Like the ones we would admire together when I was a child. She would name whatever flower I'd point a little wet finger at, *peony, bleeding heart, narcissus,* teaching me the simple language of beauty. Later, it was poetry we shared, from a big book, with trips to the unabridged dictionary as we encountered interesting words, *ineluctable, lambent, fecund*. Language is all that saves her now from a diminished life. Flowers and poetry, with one cookie every afternoon.

"Flowers don't like to open when they're being watched," she states. Nonetheless, what else is there to do? Clock ticks, curtain brushes the windowsill, an aide brings clean towels. We watch the flowers. When we look away, or blink, or nod off, they open, petal by petal, and show their hairy yellow tongues by the time a crackling loudspeaker calls the residents to lunch.

I help steer Mom's walker down the hall to the little dining room where a social drama is enacted three times a day. "My table-mates are so boring," she complains, "and I hope that new woman won't sit with us. She brags about her children. See the man with the oxygen tank? He used to be a famous psychiatrist. He was just a scrawny kid in high school Latin class," she explains, "(and he was dumb)," she whispers.

"This is my daughter," she tells everyone who wheels toward the door. One of her table-mates approaches me with a smile. "Your mother was my first crush, back in 1928 when we were 13 and skated on Norris Lake all winter long." He leans on her shoulder, and she rolls her eyes at me. Sooner or later, most of the Jews in Rochester end up here, before they arrive at Parsky's that is. And if they didn't like each other before, now they have no choice.

Not everyone goes to the dining room. Some sit in the hall under hand-made afghans, heads lolling forward. Out of respect, I restrain my stride toward the elevator so that firm feet will not rebuke them. I push the "Down" button. Wait. Wait. The pale old people watch me, watch anything new, anything that moves. Mom is still standing in the doorway of the dining room, just the way she used to stand in the front door of her house in a bathrobe as we pulled out at dawn for the long drive back to Maine. The "Down" arrow bings. She smiles and waves. The silver door slides open.

Clutching my purse, dangling the rental-car keys from one finger, I step into the elevator. Everything they've lost is still mine—money and a car, strong legs, good eyesight, freedom. I push "Lobby," but the door stays open, timed to accommodate walkers and wheelchairs and rolling carts. Mom is still watching me, all the old people are watching me, and my guilt is too intense. I can't wait any longer. I push "Close Door," and it slides across the stage-set of Mom's third-floor life. I'm alone with the quiet whirring of the elevator, and down I go.

When Joanie visits, and leaves for the lunch hour, she feels guilty to be doing all the things Mom used to love. She can't really enjoy the Art Gallery, or eating a bagel at Bruegger's, or window-shopping on Park Avenue, because she keeps thinking of Mom with her monotonous egg salad sandwich. She begs Mom to come out with her, to do the old things. But Mom's little room, her journey down the elevator for afternoon tea, are enough for her now. She is like a passenger waiting on the tarmac. I sure hope her boarding pass is valid.

Barbie leaves for the winter. Who wouldn't choose Florida over Rochester's white sky and constant snow? The rest of the year, she finds it impossible to drive by without a twinge of guilt that our mother's an old woman trapped inside this looming building, so she stops in daily.

As for me, guilt dissipates once I hit the lobby. Lunch-time is a ritual of filial homage, doing the things she taught me to enjoy. I go to Highland Park, and eat a sandwich with my back against a huge old linden at the top of a steep, grassy bowl. I can just picture Mom and her three siblings rolling down this very hill to where Gramma and Grampa sat in folding chairs with a picnic laid out on the grass. Later, Mom and Dad brought us here, especially at lilac time the middle of May. Two weeks from now, those thousand lilac bushes that dot the lower reaches of the park will bow under the fragrant weight of white, lavender, and deep purple blossoms, the original "Kodak moment" in the city that Kodak built. Not to mention the rhododendrons and azaleas with a backdrop of dark pines and ancient oaks. At the Lilac Festival, all this and a colorful pansy bed by the road will be upstaged by hot dog carts and T-shirt vendors. But for now, the intimate grove of Japanese maples, the formal row of sycamores along a black iron fence, the upstanding Australian pine and charming gingko, are more than enough splendor. People are so happy here among the plants, walking the path or roaming the grass, sitting on a bench or wherever they want, even in the crotch of an old cedar tree.

I lean back against the deeply corrugated bark, and smile. *This is all mine!* Mom gave me the gift to love trees. She'd park my carriage in the shade of a willow, or bring me lunch under a blossoming cherry. When my sisters were in school, she took me to galleries and parks, making no distinction between the beauty of art or nature. My familiar trees in Maine are first-generation roots in a new land compared to these, going back through grandparents to great-grandparents just off the boat, who made a living sewing buttons on suits at Hickey-Freeman, and spent Shabbat afternoons here. They didn't know it, but their lives and their deaths made a home for us. And now we are doing that, too, our changing lives anchored by hidden roots that crawl along in the dark gathering nourishment. And then a new shoot pops up and it's another generation, and then another. Trees are a prayer for the future. No matter how we go down, we come back up again from the root.

I stand and brush the grass off my pants, pass the giant oaks where we scattered Dad's ashes. He's not here anymore, he's way up there in the new leaves of spring. He was, in the end, mineral. And now he is vegetable. And once those squirrels get busy eating acorns, Dad will be animal again. I laugh, remembering how he used to warn us, "Don't feed the squirrels—they'll think you're nuts."

It's late afternoon, any late afternoon, and Mom is killing time before she's called to supper. She's had her tea downstairs, her one cookie. She opens a book, and swims away from the room where all that's left of her possessions is the formal photo of three smiling daughters in matching black sweaters and pearls. She turns the pages, in another world, until the phone rings, and it's me.

Some day the phone will ring and no one will answer. The final curtain of her play will be drawn. Or is it a veil? In my earliest memory I'm napping in my parents' room on Edgerton Street, watching the gauzy curtain blow in and out over the bay window, and downstairs they are reading in the living room, and my sisters are outside playing, and my whole life is in front of me. The phone rings and rings, and I hold my breath at the other end, in Maine, hoping she will answer.

The College and the Woods

It's complicated, loving trees. This is not a tree-loving world. For twenty-five years, my daily life has moved between two poles. Home is a shelter built of trees among trees, a place in the woods that invites me to look up, to listen, shaded and shaped by trees. I bring this shape to my work in the world, as a certified organic tree-hugging hippie professor.

I want the college to be a tree-loving place, too, so we can teach and learn how humans coexist with trees. Trees transform the CO_2 of all our academic talk into oxygen that allows us to keep on talking. Only the students, who spend nights on campus, get to hear trees take a turn exhaling CO_2—speaking—when the rest of us are silent. Students are the ones who absorb "the wilderness between the words," as my student Jenn put it. This story, of loving trees in a world that does not love trees, is planted for them, whose voices sprout here like tender new leaves at the crown of the tree.

Over the years, I've been one to question the cutting of this tree or that on campus. Speaking for trees has deepened my respect for their gestural, cyclical, inclusive language. Speaking for trees is not the same as speaking Tree. In Tree, All is One. Accept what is. Speaking *for* them is a polemic, an argument, a plea with grief the customary end-punctuation. Grief is not in the lexicon of Tree. But how can a human refrain from grief, when the first maple to get its lime-green flowers in spring is cut down to make way for a steam pipe? When stately firs are removed for a utility building; the last elm, gone in a weekend, replaced by a streetlamp? After an ice storm damaged the old maples lining the academic quad, they were taken down between semesters with few to witness the deed. "Limbs fall on frozen ground, protests on deaf ears," wrote Julia on a piece of bark she slipped under my office door.

There's always a reason. Reason is the death of trees. Their concentric stories radiate from the core. We mark time by linear progress, and the structure of a college provides a maze for that effort, with proper channels everywhere you turn. We push ever forward to keep up with the competition—we're about state-of-the-art facilities, winning teams, accomplished professors, diverse students.

And we're about knowledge, of course. Thoreau warns against "Useful Knowledge," and adds, "methinks there is equal need of a Society for the Diffusion of Useful Ignorance, what we will call Beautiful Knowledge...The highest we can attain to is not Knowledge, but Sympathy with Intelligence." Sympathy, alas, is not one of our precepts. Tolerance, yes, a compassion born of knowledge. But knowledge can impede "the discovery that there are more things in heaven and earth than are dreamed of in our philosophy." Sympathy erases the boundary that Knowledge draws. We have to know ledge with our roots, as trees do. We have to stand on the earth, and be still.

Befriending trees on lunch-time walks exposes me to some kind of cosmic irony, for no sooner do I get to know one, it's the next to be cut down. Not that they mind. The language of Tree says, Nothing is lost. All is Love. So how to make the case for sparing trees in a language with no "no"? Some trees make their own case. We all recognize the majestic pair of European beeches by the student union as the noblest trees on campus, planted in 1951 and nurtured through the first harsh winter with warm water on the roots. In the 1980s, the architect designed the student union to highlight the beeches with an arch that connects one side of campus to the other, reflecting the way trees connect our intellect to our spiritual selves. Their smooth grey trunks support graceful branches that reach down to raise us as we pass through. These rooted icons declare the college is here to stay, along with the first buildings (brick with copper roofs) and the new buildings (brick with copper roofs), on a hilltop overlooking the Kennebec River watershed, blue hills fading toward the sea. A few gnarly old maples were here before the college. Apple trees of a former orchard still bear fruit in what's now the Arboretum, a borderland where the college and the woods get along, a sacred space where trees teach by their presence, not by what they represent.

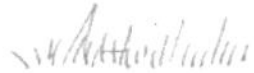

Representation is a function of our language, not theirs. We encounter a tree, leaves all glistening in the sun, and we see a metaphor—the leaves are pages, say, the tree is a book—and life drains out. The tree becomes something it is not. A tree is so real we can't say what it is. That's why I pencilled "arboretum" in the syllabus of my Critical Theory course for the week before spring break. Critical Theory argues that words build culture and identity. Maybe so. But I want to widen the context to what we know without words. By mid-semester we're worn down by words, so we leave the stale classroom that swarms with coughs, the corridor where chalk taps on blackboards behind numbered doors, the orderly bricks and rows of bare trees. I turn around to see this group of trusting English majors following me into a tangle of trees. I don't really know what I'm doing, but unpredictable nature will provide a teachable moment.

The sound of feet shushing through wet snow rises above our chatter. We come to the bridge, and, one at a time, cross the double plank with shrieks and laughter. The swift brook below us is black and white. Reconvened in silence on the other side, we hear the water's deafening roar. "Did that just start?" Lindsay exclaims. "How could we have missed it?"

I smile, thanking the brook for the moment I knew it held in store. When words fall away, contrary to what critical theorists propose, there is a presence, not merely an absence. While we read, sleep, eat, and get older, a brook's life goes on. All of us together are the living presence that is the natural world. We don't have to say a thing to make it happen.

We proceed along the rocky path to a cluster of hemlocks. Trunks rise and branches interlace overhead, roots grip the earth, which gives me the next idea. "Form a circle," I say, "and hold hands." A pulse travels around the circle. We all feel it. "Is that coming from the trees?" Abigail whispers. We lean way back and bend our knees. Eyes point straight up at bleak sky. "This is how a treetop sees," says Erin. Wind ruffles the hemlock boughs. By now we're quiet enough to hear it the first time.

Next day, in a circle of one-arm chairs, we're back to literary theory. No holding hands today. Raise hands, maybe. Mine are white with chalk as I introduce phenomenology, the theory of how we mold our perceptions into knowledge—how we make sense of what we read.

"You're not just a passive reader," I explain. "You're the builder, because description can't show you an actual object. The words are only a blueprint." Blank faces. I write "phenomenology" on the board. They copy it in their notebooks.

"Take yesterday. The mention of a brook in literature requires your experience of real brooks in nature, how they swirl and throw mist in your face. We can only animate the novelist's rushing brook if we're alive to the world."

"Brooks are easy. But how are we supposed to imagine the lives of these characters?" asks Andrew, waving his copy of Russell Banks' *Affliction* over his head. "I was never a poor, unemployed, divorced guy in a stinking trailer with a leaky roof. Isn't it up to Banks to tell me everything I need to know?"

"He can't give you everything," says Jared. "You have to leap from what you know to what you don't know." I nod and write "hermeneutic circle" on the board, turn around and see only the top of heads as they bow to copy it down.

"Knowledge is an exchange of words," I say when they look up. "Hermeneutics is how we place new knowledge into the context of what we already know. That's how description works in literature." I peck "hermeneutic" with the chalk, and wonder about the other kind of knowledge. Things we just know, like fear, intuition, compassion, love.

"Look, I've never been inside a trailer," insists Andrew. "Here we are, in this well-maintained college where everything's in order. We have an expectation that our lives..." Suddenly, overhead, water gurgles violently in the pipes. Pipes I've never noticed before, with a pressure valve right over my seat. Andrew's voice stops and we raise our eyes to the ceiling. When streams talk, we listen. That much we learned yesterday.

...whoosh, glink, clang, pfffffff... Slowly, the valve leaks a drop on the carpet by my foot. Another drop hits Ryan's notebook. He pushes back his chair. Melisse's pack receives the next drop.

...glurk, FFFFFF, sshhhhhHHHHHHH... We disrupt the circle and flee down the hall past classrooms where the word exchange continues unabated. The unpredictable is a good teacher. What we can't imagine springs us from what we think we know.

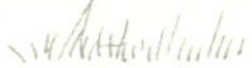

A moment is not just a minute. A moment is a space in which something important happens, something momentous, something that builds momentum. We live in our imagination, a nation of images where no word stands alone, but gathers meaning from memory, experience, dream. Untangle the word "tree" from this inner community. Observe a tree and learn the core lesson of life: Things are what they are. Now.

Chris says trees showed him the secret of solitude within community, not by metaphor but by the way they live. Students live packed together in dorms and classrooms, dining hall, library, lab, locker room. He quickly recognized the assignment in Land and Language—go find a tree and make it yours by writing under it—as a chance to listen to himself. Trees speak by saying back what we're thinking. Our words sound wiser when exhaled by a tree. Leaning against the trunk, asking "What should I do?," human and tree breathe together, alone, like meditating monks.

The tree holds cyclical time in its branches, while college time ticks forward and there's never enough of it. The library clock-tower's four faces watch us stream across campus every hour on the hour, to classrooms where another clock looms over the professor's head. The chapel bells chime quarter-hours. Papers are due when they're due, or else they are late. Fourteen weeks, and then the exam. Time holds us in community. We need each other to make this college run.

Chris is right, there is no solitude without community, even on a quiet lunch-time walk. The library tower is the pin, and I am hands revolving around the pond, tick-tock, fifteen minutes by the clock. Lose track of time at the willow tree where students gave spring presentations the year I was waiting for Dad to die. Stop to check mushrooms thick in the grass. Look up to see the next clock face peering over my shoulder, and I'm late, quick-quack, got to get back. Water shimmers, willows wave. Third face urges me up the stairs to my office where red message light blinks, computer hums. Grab briefcase. Fourth face presses my back as I run across the quad to class.

The clock is always watching. There's no escape, unless I walk farther, up the hill behind the buildings, beyond college time. Crickets rule. Mountains and horizon blue in the distance, ledge outcrop underfoot. Sit on parched grass, find a few clover or yarrow leaves in the thatch to chew on. Lie back. Blue sky, warm sun. Doze. Chapel chimes three-quarters. Stand up quick. Brush off pants. Scurry down to class with a twig in my hair.

Sometimes we walk up the hill as a class, to experience the land as teacher. One early April day, thick slabs of old snow on the dun grass, we climb to see in all directions. I say, "Imagine your past as a bubble behind you, your future a bubble in front. Feel yourself as the dot between." We stand in silence and the minutes get big and become a moment. Wind in bare oak branches, a single bird, hum of distant highway. We stand there so long that a sudden snow squall coats us in white. Liz, graduating soon, breaks the silence. She moans, "My future bubble is empty!" We all laugh as we stand on the circle of bare grass our presence left in the quick snowfall. The chime sounds from below, and class is over.

There is no solitude without the larger scheme. We walk down to campus, passing under the two enormous beech trees steady amid the constant motion of campus life. They grow from the heart. We pass under snow-tufted branches and become part of their living layer. The heart is life itself, all present unbroken circle ascending descending. This is not a metaphor. This is Love.

Love is easy on a beautiful May day, last class meeting under the beech trees, final papers handed in. Beeches write their story in leaves that turn gold in October, leathery in November, then cling to the branches all winter long, rattling in the wind, whispering snow, dripping ice. The leaves become bleached and thin, nothing but fairy-skin and veins, still holding on against April gusts. On this breezy day the trees, too, are finally letting go of their papery leaves. We scatter with good-byes from under the branches where buds sharpen like pencils and unfold into fuzzy green brushes that write the joy of earth.

I'm left holding a stack of papers, pages of words to sum up a semester of words. It's easy to love such words, and to think you've learned the lessons. But this is only the paper. This is not the test. The test comes when you look Love in the eye. Love is not a word. Love is a tough gnarl, a solid burl. There is no edge to get under, no way to lift it out and examine it, no evidence for and against it, no etiology nor teleology, no -ology at all. Love Is.

The next fall, picking up the campus newspaper, I know it when I see it. This is the test. Headline announces proposed addition to student union. And here's the architect's drawing. I take a look—food court, game room, pub, grand staircase, ...coffee bar?...right there?...where one of the beech trees stands?—

I go into my office and close the door. In the hall there's a lot of excitement, today being the 2004 presidential election, and George W. Bush is in a tight race against John Kerry. I'm deaf to everything but the threatened tree. Slump down in a chair and tumble right to sorrow. Rage is useless. I know that much, as one who speaks for trees, crying *Why?* to those who decide, being dismissed with a reason. Face it, that tree is as good as dead.

The words "decide" and "deciduous" share a root that means "fall, kill, cut to pieces." *Deciduous* is a tree that drops its leaves. *Decide* is a verb that can drop a whole tree. *Decide* is deicide, if you worship trees. My heart plunges like a stone to someplace below my knees. Remind me again of the lesson I thought I'd finally learned?—to stop grieving for every lost tree, to cherish what remains, until the merest sliver of wood will keep me afloat? The chapel chimes quarter-to. I toss the newspaper aside and gather my books. Head for class. Be the teacher. Act the part. While we're writing in our journals, I stare at the trunk of a maple tree just outside, one of the few old trees left from pasture days. Its knobby girth fills the window, with only the gable of the President's House visible beyond a nearly bare branch. Oh, tree, what should I do?

A dead leaf quivers in the November wind. *Leaf,* it whispers through the windowpane. Really? Leave?

I call the class together and we close our journals. Am I going to leave the college over a beech tree? It's true I'd always joked if they go, I go. And now the maple is giving me the same advice. But will that help save the tree? Another quick glance at the maple trunk. This time it says, *Bark*.

Night. I'm home alone, hunched next to the kitchen woodstove listening to early election returns. Even the good news doesn't dissolve my mute despair. Bush is losing. The house is dark except for the little green dot on the radio dial. The outline of black pines against a deep sapphire sky fills the window. It's easier to hear what trees have to say at night—big porous words honeycombed with possibility. *Bark*, the maple had said this afternoon. *Yes, bark!* the trusted home-pines repeat. My spine straightens—I can do something about this! If I don't, the old beech will definitely be cut down. If I bark about it, there's at least a chance. That tree is not dead yet.

I start scribbling a letter to like-minded colleagues. To the college president. To the building committee. I don't like to just complain, so I sketch some alternative designs that would leave room for both trees. I'm getting excited about this chance to help the college and the woods get along. Maybe the maple was right, maybe I should leave. But first I will bark. Speaking Tree to power will be my legacy.

I stop paying attention to the radio as I write and draw late into the night. This time, instead of waiting until the tree is gone to cry *Why?*—and the answer is never enough—I will pre-empt grief with action. George W. Bush is now just barely winning over John Kerry. The sudden shift in the returns ought to tell me something about the vagaries of hope, but I'm too busy saving a tree to notice.

Bush won a second term, and the war in Iraq rages on. Meanwhile I'm learning the ways of politics from a tree. The beech fight will take more than barking, and the maple outside of Runnals 110 continues to coach me through the window while we're all writing in our journals. *Branch*, it says. My letter stirs other colleagues who depend on old trees for balance. Someone else steps up to help, and with two passionate professors pooling words and strategy, we branch out into a community of vociferous tree-lovers. We become Friends of the Beeches, with a web site for background and alternatives, an on-line petition, and a growing network. Next thing I know, having been advised by the maple to *Stump*, Jim and I are standing at the front of the faculty meeting, presenting a motion to spare both beech trees. Jim is handing a petition to the President, signed by a majority of faculty and a quarter of the students. My heart is pounding as I address our colleagues because I know professors all too well. We're trained to be skeptical of passion, to demand logical evidence. And here I am, professing my belief that education is rooted in the land, that a college can teach by considering its place in nature. They actually listen to what Jim and I are saying, and they vote Yes to the motion, with just a few abstentions from administrators. Yes, we should spare both beech trees, even if it means making the coffee bar smaller.

As I leave the jubilant meeting and step out into the cold December evening, a defeatist question creeps up on me—What just happened? We overwhelmingly passed a sense-of-the-faculty motion, and it will go into the minutes. Minutes are a record of how a college runs, the tick-tick-tick of our clockwork. But I know it's not the faculty's role to decide about building plans. A college does what it wants, what it can, what it has to do, and is not ruled by values that perhaps only an individual can hold. I do not wish to speak here of minutes but of moments, the kind where the sky opens up and truth drops on you and you're compelled to act. The minutes show that two professors proposed a motion and we voted on it. Only the moments can tell this story of love and transformation.

It's winter break. The tree still lives. More and more, I'm thinking about resigning, not that it would do any good, and it would be hard to articulate what I'm protesting. Resigning because of a single tree, in a world that chops them down every day? And it's not as if Kal and I never cut down a tree. I'm not blind to the contradictions of being human within the natural world, where we do silly things like build a solar house surrounded by woods. When we first arrived, we guyed our tent to a little oak sapling. It grew lush and strong outside Noah's window as he grew on the inside. Finally the oak was shading our solar panels. Reluctantly we cut it down. Its twenty-nine rings revealed that it sprouted from an acorn the year we were married. We planted daffodils around the stump, and used the wood for heat. The issue isn't whether you cut down a tree or not. It's about respecting roots, and making every effort to get along with plants who have as much right to live as we do. I find it hard to teach how to be a good citizen of the planet, at a college that strives to be "green" in so many important ways, but not at the root.

The beech tree, bare and innocent by the archway of the student union, not knowing or caring that other colleges have better student unions, does not cry, "Save me!" Instead, it offers me the greenest lesson on how to love trees in a world that does not. *Stay. Defend what you love. And if you lose, go down with dignity.* Once again in my life, a tree is trying to save me. And this is the very reason I'm trying to save it.

And so our fight continues. Some want dramatic protests, street theater, banners and leaflets, tree-sitting or chaining ourselves to the trunk. If students would only do that. But the student newspaper opines that a tree is just a tree, whereas the biggest possible student union would improve campus life. We faculty shape our protest along proper channels, starting with the President. But he likes proper channels, too, and diverts us to the building committee. They will not meet with us. Our petition lies buried in the minutes of the December faculty meeting, a copy entombed in the library's special collection. Surely the Trustees will listen. I write them a letter, but discover their addresses are not public information. By brash moves, I manage to get a memo from Friends of the Beeches into the packet they'll receive at their January meeting. But they like proper channels, too, and nothing comes of it, neither a minute nor a moment. We continue to make noise until the college hires an arborist to assess the tree—it's healthy, it's rare—so the excuse that it's sick proves untrue. The committee agrees to send our letter to the architect, asking him to submit alternative designs. They invite him back to campus to hear our concerns. We're getting somewhere!

Meanwhile, I'm peppering the President with e-mails. He's a philosopher, and his thoughtful answers coalesce into a discussion about nature and people—Is there really an inherent distinction between the natural environment and the built one? Isn't a campus landscape, after all, a built environment? Isn't almost every place on earth in some way built, including wilderness that we designate as such? I have a growing hunch he's a man who agrees about the tree, someone I can call friend. But he's a president who picks his battles. He's going to leave this decision to the committee.

The architect comes on the Ides of March. His defense against a hostile crowd is to tell us stories about all the trees he's saved in his career. He clearly favors his original design, and the alternatives he presents are simply cut-back versions of it. He talks about "trade-offs"—we can have the space for everything we want...or we can have less than we want, and keep an old tree that might not even live very long. I drive home with a stone in my belly. "You guys've been had," says Kal. The very next day the committee makes its decision in closed session, and we all leave campus for spring break.

Day after break. Miserable wet snow, low sky. The President has asked for a meeting with me and Jim. We figure the fight is over. We've decided to "be nice" and just take whatever he tells us. Jim wears a black suit—"I have a funeral kind of feeling," he mutters as we enter the inner sanctum. But we're still pretending the President is going to create an endowed chair in Biophilia for us. He's going to thank us for saving the college from cutting off its roots.

"I've accepted the committee's recommendation," he says, closing the cherry-panelled door and taking his seat in a wing chair. We're holding our breath. He straightens his tie. His clock strikes twelve. "They chose the original plan." He pierces us with a blue-eyed look from under his brows. "I'm sorry."

Outside the window, noon is erased by dark snow. I sink inside myself, numb. Be nice. Talk for an hour. Don't argue anymore, or maybe just a little. I've come to like the guy, and understand that he separates his own values from his role as president. He's an orb. If you push with muscular strength, he rolls away. I thought I'd learned the trick, to be a branch pressing on a neighboring branch with the force of growth. That might work with the man, but the President kept rolling, and we never stood a chance.

Cordial handshakes. Good little professors. Thank you, thank you. As soon as we hit the stairwell, we're angry.

The tree still lives, and continues to teach me what love really is—advocacy without holding on, and forgiveness. You have to be broken-hearted in order to change, says my student Christina. I defended what I love, and made my usual mistake of expecting to be heard. Cassandra again. When will I ever learn? Only on the day cynicism completely blots out my innocent hope and vision. I'm still asking, can the college and the woods ever get along? But in the end, it's not about the college. It's not about the woods. It's not even about speaking Tree to power. Because how does a tree speak to power? It stands there. It lets power do all the talking. I guess I really don't know Tree at all.

There's solace in knowing you did what you could. Come spring, the Land and Language class does a circumambulation of the trees. We pour out of the building into the bright new sun, carrying Gary Snyder's *Mountains and Rivers without End*. We select the oldest trees on campus, and under each one we stop to read a poem. John chooses "Earth Verse" for the old maple by the classroom window:

Wide enough to keep you looking
Open enough to keep you moving
Dry enough to keep you honest
Green enough to go on living
Old enough to give you dreams

We move on, and arrive at the two beeches. Twenty of us stoop to get under the doomed tree (even the President calls it that, to me). Its branches swell with pencil-point buds. We're astonished by the clawfoot roots, the trunk so broad it blocks our view of each other. There's a microclimate under here, mossy ground-cover, sweetly moist, and the voice of ten-thousand silky new leaves melts college time away. Beth chooses to read "Mā," a mother's newsy letter to her son about the trivia of daily life—who died, how the crops are doing, don't drink too much. "What does this poem have to do with a tree?" I ask, not knowing the answer. Hanna says, "It's all about the strivings and desires of human life, which is what causes trees like this to be cut down." We lay our hands on smooth grey bark, touch the velvety cushion of moss growing where the trunk splits in two.

Squatting under high bushes one hot summer day, blueberries going *plink-plink* into a bucket, I think about the President, who told me he grows blueberry bushes at his lake house. I could hate the college, hate the decision, hate him for not stopping it. But the tree still lives, and hate is not one of its lessons. Each leaf has its own small life to lead, and the tree stands, like a college with all its passing people. Like nature, with all its passing trees. Our fight was a clash of values that could have erupted over any number of college decisions that some faculty and students disagree with. It all centered around a tree, but probed deeply to the root of priorities, process, image, attitude. In a sense it was a safe mission, because who can fault defending a tree? It was not, many say, a failed mission, and I'm sure the tree would agree.

So, not having made any enemies (thanks to Tree guidance), and in fact having made a friend, here I am walking under the two beeches and into the student union to meet the President for lunch this first week of September. Construction will begin next spring. The test will be to love the doomed tree until they cut it down. He and I agreed to find a new topic, so we sit in a booth with tuna sandwiches, talking about blueberry bushes and pear trees. Our old topic, in a new way. "I have an apple tree," he says, "over at the President's House. Come pick some."

I go there after work. He's still at his office, and I feel a little funny being in his yard. He left a long-handled picker leaning against the apple tree for everyone to use, but the aroma rising like sweet steam off the fallen fruit beckons me to get down and scoop drops into a bag. The five o'clock chime makes me think back over all the old bitterness I've tasted in my years here, wanting the college—nay, the world—to think the way I do. Maybe you can only change people by accepting who they are. And you become changed in the process. Neighboring branches accommodate each other's growth. We all want to bear fruit. I stand up and crunch my teeth into a juicy apple. I'm finally learning to speak Tree.

The beech tree went down, with dignity, on January 19, 2006. Long live the tree.

After

Long lives the tree. Its root is one with all roots, one with the earth and everything that lives on this planet. Some of us who live are watching *An Inconvenient Truth* on this Saturday afternoon as we whirl around the sun, our seats bolted to the sloped floor of the Colonial Theater in Belfast, Maine.

The credits roll, and the "what you can do" conclusion of the movie. Behind my eyes, I'm still seeing Al Gore's dappled childhood river. I'm seeing what he loves, what he's rooted in, where his passion comes from.

And I'm still seeing the beech tree's silvery branches, wood chips now.

Earth in the balance, out of balance because individuals and institutions don't base decisions on the same set of values. We ask, standing by our childhood rivers, how will this affect my life, my children's life? Institutions don't go down to the river. They have no childhood, no children. They forget they are made of people.

I have accepted that difference as a matter of fact: institutions, corporations, governments operate on a different scale. But now a thought surges up my spine as I sit, bolted and whirling, in the dark theater ...THAT DIFFERENCE IS EXACTLY THE PROBLEM.

I rise from my seat to step out into the humid late afternoon, June thunderstorms all cleared away. I'm seeing the little stone bridge where I tumbled into the flood, the maples who watched me get out. Treetop vision—*That is so*—urged me to accept what is. Which doesn't mean do nothing, I now see. Accept *and* defend. Love, *and* be furious if that's what gets you moving. Tree-hugger. Madwoman. It's all a bridge to be crossed back and forth as long as we have voice and vision.